Carmel and Music

Simon Nolan, O. Carm.

CARMELITE MEDIA

Edited and Layout by William J. Harry, O. Carm.

Copyright © 2020

Printed and bound in the United States of America

Current Printed Edition ISBN: 978-1-936742-18-9
E-Book ISBN: 978-1-936742-19-6

In memory of my father

Brian Nolan
(1943-2018)

Detail of the *Squarcialupi Codex*, a beautifully decorated music manuscript depicting Bartolino da Padova (from Padua, Italy) in his Carmelite brown habit and white mantle. The full page from the Codex is reproduced on page 5.

Table of Contents

Introduction

This book is an invitation to explore the theme of Carmel and music. In some cases, it deals with Carmelites who were themselves musicians and composers such as Bartolino da Padova, John Hothby, Giovanni Bonadies, Manuel Cardoso, Benedictus Buns and Hermann Cohen, all of whom are receiving greater attention in recent years and are included in this volume. In other cases, Carmelite history, spirituality or even a particular Carmelite have been an inspiration to major composers such as Francis Poulenc, Sir Lennox Berkeley and Sir John Tavener. George Frederick Handel composed music for the Feast of Our Lady of Mount Carmel on foot of a commission. Felix Mendelssohn's oratorio *Elijah* may be justifiably brought into the discussion based as it is on the Biblical account of Elijah, Prophet of Carmel.

There is always something a little strange about writing on the topic of music since music is primarily sound, something to be played, something to be listened to. But words can nudge us in the right direction and act as helpful signposts to assist us in our exploration of the music. As an aid to the reader's listening, a list of available recordings is provided at the end of the volume.

This book does not pretend to be comprehensive. The major figures and major works are covered but there are others worthy of attention. For example, the Flemish Carmelite organist and composer, Lambert Chaumont (c.1630-1712), was a significant figure whose music is sometimes played and recorded today. In addition to Lennox Berkeley's *Four Poems of Saint Teresa of Avila*, dealt with here, some attention could be paid to the work of another English composer, Edmund Rubbra (1901-1986), and his very fine *Mass in Honour of Saint Teresa of Avila*. A focus of this book is Francis Poulenc's opera, *Dialogues des Carmélites*; the *Suite Carmelite* for organ by French composer, Jean Françaix (1912-1997), is similarly inspired by the story of the Carmelite nuns of Compiègne, although not studied here. There are undoubtedly other historical Carmelite centres of music besides those of Mantua, Bruges, Augsburg and Boxmeer which are included in this book: Naples, for example. There exist, therefore, opportunities for further work in the future. Finally, there is a living tradition within the Carmelite family today and an ongoing narrative of Carmel and music across many continents, in churches, friaries, formation houses, parishes and schools, involving many different peoples and different musical and cultural traditions. Again, it is to be hoped that a work such as this may inspire Carmelites and those associated with them to reflect on the important role music has in our lives.

This is not a work of musicology or academic music history. For the most part technical jargon is avoided or at least explained. The book is intended, primarily, for the general reader who is interested in exploring the topic of Carmel and music. It makes no grand conclusions about music and spirituality or about there being any peculiarly musical character to the Carmelite charism. However, it is remarkable that the Carmelite Order has produced several musicians of world standing and that its rich history and spirituality has been such an inspiration to first-rate composers in various ages. Music and spirituality have long been associated in the philosophies of the ancients and in various world religions up to the present day. Music does seem to open our ears onto the transcendent and it does have the power to go deep within the heart and would appear, therefore, to go very well with the Carmelite charism with its emphasis on meeting God and the journey within. Among the saints and blesseds of the Carmelite family, Blessed John of Saint Samson, the leading spiritual figure of the reform of Touraine, was a very accomplished organist, as well as playing the spinet, the harp, the lute, the flute, and the oboe. Saint Elizabeth of the Trinity was a talented conservatory-trained pianist with great potential for developing a career as a recitalist.

My thanks are due to a number of people without whom this volume would not have come to be. The late Redemptus Valabek, O. Carm., first suggested I write a series of articles for *Carmel in the World* on Carmel and music. The late Arie Kallenberg introduced me to Benedictus of Saint Joseph (Buns), O. Carm., kindly sending me recordings of the Carmelite composer's work. As well as encouraging my work in a general way, the late Joachim Smet, O. Carm., drew my attention to the work of John Hothby, O. Carm.; James Eivers, O. Carm., introduced me to the life and work of Father Hermann Cohen, OCD; it has been a pleasure to collaborate with him on a number of musical projects. The late Patrick McMahon, O. Carm., was a constant support as a friend and in his roles both as *praeses* of the *Institutum Carmelitanum* and editor of *Carmel in the World*. I thank Ruth Long, librarian at Gort Muire, Dublin, for her help and, above all, for introducing me to the Ghent Choir Books. I am indebted to Patrick Mullins, O. Carm., for his help with the *Kilcormac Missal* and in helping me clarify various points of Carmelite history and spirituality. I am grateful to P.J. Breen, O. Carm., editor of *Carmel in the World* for his support and to Martin Baxter, O. Carm., for his willingness to listen as I rehearsed aspects of this book. I thank the Very Revd

William J. Harry, O. Carm., former Prior Provincial of the Province of the Most Pure Heart of Mary, for encouraging me a number of years ago to gather my material into book form and for agreeing to publish it.

Simon Nolan, O. Carm.
Carmelite Priory
Whitefriar Street - Dublin
August 2020

1

Carmel and Music in the Middle Ages and Renaissance

The Beginnings of the Carmelite Order[1]

The origins of the Carmelite Order are to be traced to the very end of the twelfth and the beginning of the thirteenth centuries. Following the lead of hermits from both the Greek and Latin traditions, who had for centuries gravitated to Mount Carmel in Israel, the early Carmelites established themselves in small cells there. They were for the most part brothers, although some of their number were ordained priests. They were not locals but Latins who had come to the Holy Land, as soldiers, as pilgrims, as merchants, or as sailors. They may not have had a founder in the conventional sense but they more and more regarded the Prophet Elijah as their inspiration and patron, settling as they did near a well associated with the fiery prophet of Carmel who came to know God in the sound of sheer silence. These early Carmelite hermits lived a simple life, based on prayer and solitude, and yet celebrating the Eucharist together was essential to them, as was coming together to discuss the issues which arose from a life lived in common. Their chapel was named after Our Lady and she, along with Elijah, becomes their protector, the one they called the Lady of the Place. As representatives of the eremitical tradition, the early Carmelites on Mount Carmel co-existed with other groups of hermits and with monastic and mendicant communities: the Premonstratensians, Benedictine men and women, Franciscans, and Dominicans had all established communities in the Holy Land.[2]

As the new community consolidated itself, they were keen to obtain some level of ecclesial recognition and approval. The hermits made representation to Albert Avogadro, Patriarch of Jerusalem. Some time between 1206 and 1214 Albert composed a *"formula of life"* (*vitae formula*) for them based on how they were already living, a simple rule

---

1. For the early history of the Carmelite Order see Joachim Smet, O. Carm., *The Carmelites: A History of the Brothers of Our Lady of Mount Carmel*, Vol. 1: "Ca. 1200 until The Council of Trent," revised edition (Darien IL: Carmelite Spiritual Center, 1988). Also Joachim Smet, O. Carm. "The Carmelite Rule after 750 Years" in *Carmelus* 44 (1997), fasc. 1, pp. 21-47 and Leopold Gluekert, O. Carm., *Desert Springs in the City: A Concise History of the Carmelites* (Darien IL, Carmelite Media: 2012).
2. See Smet, "The Carmelite Rule."

steeped in Scripture, practical and yet inspiring, ending with an appeal
to common sense. As the Latin position in the Near East deteriorated,
these Carmelite recluses began to migrate westward to Europe, starting
around 1238, coming to Les Aygalades in France, to Cyprus, Sicily and
to England by 1242.[3] For a period, until 1291, the Carmelites continued to maintain a presence on Mount Carmel until they were driven out
by the Saracens. Those who migrated were outsiders when they came to
Europe, even though Europe was where most of them had originated.
Their otherness was heightened by their very strange garb: their black-
and-white striped cloaks. When young Carmelites started to attend the
newly founded universities in the late thirteenth century, the constant
teasing on the part of their fellow students soon led to them to petition
to change to a plain white cloak. And so, the Carmelites rebranded and
became thereafter the Whitefriars.

Early Carmelite Chant[4]

There is little indication as to the musical life of the first Carmelites
on Mount Carmel. The solitary lifestyle, as it is reflected in the early
version of the Rule of Saint Albert, meant that psalms were recited by
the hermits in their cells, with little opportunity for development of
community singing of the Psalter. We know little about what was sung
at the celebration of the Eucharist on Mount Carmel. Liturgical custom
dictated that Eucharist be celebrated according to the local rite: the Rite
of the Holy Sepulchre.[5] From our knowledge concerning that rite, we
can gain some clues as to the kind and style of music which obtained
in the cultural milieu out of which the Carmelites emerged.[6] We do not
know whether the early Carmelites had musical instruments. Initially, as
envisaged by Albert's document and in contrast to the celebration of the
Eucharist, the Divine Office was a private devotion which nevertheless
found its place within a community context.

The revision of the *vitae formula* of Albert by Pope Innocent IV in
1247, and his solemn approval of it as a true and proper rule (*regula
bullata*) on 1 October that year, is a defining moment. Several aspects

3.   See Bede Edwards, OCD, and Hugh Clarke, O. Carm., *The Rule of Saint Albert* (Aylesford
and Kensington: 1973), p. 21.
4.   Our knowledge of early Carmelite chant comes from the pioneering research of the leading
Carmelite musicologist, the late James Boyce, O. Carm. See James Boyce, O. Carm., *Praising God in
Carmel: Studies in Carmelite Liturgy* (Washington DC: The Carmelite Institute, 1999)
5.   The Rite of the Holy Sepulchre was developed after the crusaders took control of Jerusalem (in
July 1099) by the French clergy who took the contemporary liturgical practice at Paris as their model.
6.   See, for example, the recording *Le Chant des Templiers* by Marcel Pérès with Ensemble Organum
(see list of recordings at the end of this volume for details).

of Albert's foundational document were changed to accommodate it to the mendicant tradition already established in the West by groups such as the Franciscan and Dominican friars. From a musical point of view, the most significant change was the move towards communal celebration of the Liturgy of the Hours. From now on the Divine Office would be celebrated by the Carmelites in choir, as a group, rather than individually in each hermit's cell.

The medieval choir books of the Order, the content of which sometimes reflects the era before 1291 when the Carmelites continued to live on Mount Carmel as well as moving further afield, witness to the emergence of a musical tradition. The most important choir books of the Order still in existence today are from Mainz, Florence, Pisa and Kraków. [7] The production of choir books facilitated the singing of the Office in community. The evidence is that Carmelites took great care in producing books of liturgical texts with accompanying musical notation and we begin to notice preferences they had for certain melodies. A melody could have a unifying effect when, for example, it was used for a number of feasts of Our Lady. Melody could, therefore, appeal to the imagination, to mind, to heart and to memory and help associate one liturgical celebration with another. Oftentimes it would appear that words and music were neither original nor unique to the Carmelites but were frequently creatively adapted by the Order. The earliest Carmelite sources for music and the liturgy witness to the immense care that was taken in copying and passing on musical resources which had early on appealed to the Carmelite musical imagination.

Two early examples of Carmelite chant worth mentioning are the *Regem patriarcharum* and the *Hec est regina*. The antiphon *Regem patriarcharum* (King of Patriarchs) soon became a Carmelite favourite for the celebration of the feast of the Old Testament patriarchs, Abraham, Isaac and Jacob, on 6 October. This feast was unique to the Carmelite and Holy Sepulchre liturgies, not being celebrated in the Western Church. James Boyce notes: *The feast, directly associated with customs of the Holy Land, highlighted the eastern origins of the Carmelites and accentuated the distinctiveness of their liturgical tradition.*[8] The antiphon *Hec est regina* (This is the Queen) was sung as part of Vespers on the feasts of the Annunciation and the Conception of the Virgin Mary. It is likely

---

7.   The Carmelite choir books of Mainz date from the 1430s, of Florence from the end of the fourteenth century, of Pisa from 1312-1342 and of Kraków from 1397 up to the nineteenth century. See James Boyce, O. Carm., *op. cit.*, pp. 1-45.

8.   James Boyce, O. Carm., *op. cit.*, p. 253. An antiphon is a short text sung before the chanting of a psalm or canticle in the Divine Office (and usually repeated at the end).

both the text and music came from the liturgy of the Knights Templar.[9] Looking at the occurrence of these two chants in the medieval choir books, what is remarkable is the care taken by the Carmelites to preserve the contours of the melodies they adopted and adapted across the celebration of various feasts and from one locale to another.

In general musical terms, it is worth noting two things about these medieval Carmelite chants. First, in both cases the music is *monophonic*: there is a single melody without harmony or any additional melody line running along with it (known as *counterpoint*). Much medieval music has this monophonic character and is to be contrasted stylistically with the polyphonic music which also existed in the period.[10] Secondly, each antiphon is of a different *mode*: technically, the *Regem patriarcharum* is in mode 4 and the *Hec est regina* is in mode 1. The system of modes dominated the theory and practice of music in the medieval West (its roots were in ancient antiquity). A mode is a particular set of musical notes forming a scale from which melodies are drawn. A modern musician in the West will think in terms of major and minor keys. In the Middle Ages a musician thought in terms of modes: particular modes provided particular sets of notes from which melodies could be derived. Much as with different major and minor keys today, different modes were considered to have different characters, moods or colours and, accordingly, to have different effects on listeners.

It is worth mentioning a particular feature of the *Hec est regina*. The chant takes the form of a prayer of intercession which recalls Mary's role in reconciling humanity to God. The melody serves to emphasise the salvific import of the words: for example, the note *d* occurs along with the words *virginem* (virgin), *regem* (king), *hominem* (man), and *nobis omnibus* (for us all).

Bartolino da Padova, O. Carm. (fl. 1381-1410)[11]

As a relatively early figure, there are very few facts known about Bartolino da Padova (from Padua, Italy). We have the surviving works which bear his name. We know he was a Carmelite from his depiction in the famous *Squarcialupi Codex*, a beautiful decorated music manuscript which shows Bartolino in his brown habit and white mantle.

9. Or perhaps the Knights Templar and the Carmelites had a common source for the antiphon.
10. Polyphony is the musical style of simultaneously combining a number of parts, each forming an individual melody and harmonizing with each other. A prime example of advanced polyphonic compositional style is the music of the Carmelite composer, Frei Manuel Cardoso, O. Carm. (see Chapter 2).
11. For the life and works of Bartolino da Padova, O. Carm., see "Bartolino da Padova" at *Grove Music Online* (www.oxfordmusiconline.com).

A page of the *Squarcialupi Codex* a highly illuminated music manuscript showing Carmelite Bartolino da Padova, in his brown Carmelite habit and white mantle. The Codex is the single largest primary source of music of the 14th-century, Italian Trecento.

Elsewhere, in a manuscript at Modena, a work of Bartolino's is marked "Frater Carmelitus."

There has been some scholarly debate as to whether Bartolino remained in his native Padua or whether he also worked at Florence; his works were popular in Tuscany at the time. He was most famous as a composer of madrigals[12] and the surviving examples were often written for specific occasions and allude to contemporary personages. Bartolino would appear to have been employed by the noble Carrara family who were Lords of Padua. References to the Visconti family (dukes of Milan) in his work are difficult to interpret. It has been suggested that Bartolino could have accompanied Gian Galeazzo Visconti (1351-1402) on his campaigns in northern Italy (which would have included Padua). However, some scholars think Bartolino may have been satirising the Viscontis and declaring his support for the Carraras.

Bartolino's style of composition was influenced by the composer Jacopo da Bologna (mentioned below in connection with the *Codex Faenza*). This is seen in the way in which the Carmelite composer links lines in his madrigals and in the way he changes the metre in the refrains in the same works. While Bartolino is very Italian in the way he writes his music, there are also clear French influences on his work. In a work such as *Alba Columba* (White dove) he follows the French practice of accompanying the high voice with countertenor and tenor. The more Italian approach of Jacopo would usually employ two upper voices set against a tenor part. Interestingly, *Alba Columba*, refers to the motto and emblem of the Viscontis. Again, depending on which side one takes in the scholarly debate, Bartolino is being either satirical or laudatory here.

John Hothby (Johannes Octoboni), O. Carm. (c. 1430-1487)[13]

John Hothby was an English Carmelite composer and musical theorist. Before settling in Lucca, Italy, at the Cathedral of San Martino in February 1467, Hothby travelled widely throughout Italy, Germany, France, Great Britain, and Spain. He made acquaintance with Lorenzo de'Medici on a visit to Florence.

Hothby was held in very high regard at Lucca both at the cathedral

---

12.   The term *madrigal* can mean different things in different eras of the history of music. In the context of Bartolino da Padova, a madrigal is to be understood as a poetic and musical form which emerged in fourteenth century Italy, with a two- or three-line verse and a one- or two-line refrain. Most madrigals of this kind are written for two vocal lines, more rarely for three voices. Bartolino also wrote *ballate*: a *ballata* (as the name suggests) was a kind of dance song where an opening and closing refrain frame stanzas which close with a repetition of the refrain.

13.   For the life and works of John Hothby, O. Carm., see "Hothby, John" at *Grove Music Online* (www.oxfordmusiconline.com). Also Pedro Memelsdorff, "John Hothby, Lorenzo il Magnifico e Robert Morton in una nuova fonte manoscritta a Mantova" in *Acta Musicologica* 78, fasc. 1 (2006), pp. 1-32; James Haar and John Nádas, "Johannes de Anglia (John Hothby): Notes on His Career In Italy" In *Acta Musicologica* 79, fasc. 2 (2007), pp. 291-358; and Benjamin Brand, "A Medieval Scholasticus and Renaissance Choirmaster: A Portrait of John Hothby at Lucca" in *Renaissance Quarterly* 63, 3 (2010), pp. 754-806.

and by the civic authorities. A sign of this is the increase in salary grant-ed him in 1469, seemingly in case he might be enticed away by those who might have sought to secure his services elsewhere. The same year the Carmelite composer was referred to as a *lector* (or teacher) in sacred theology. He also taught grammar and mathematics at Lucca. Hothby travelled to his native England at the request of Henry VII. He died in October or November 1487 in Brittany (northern France) while on his return journey to Lucca.

Hothby wrote a large number of treatises on music. They are for the most part highly technical, addressing the modes, the theory and prac-tice of writing music in musical notation, counterpoint, musical scales, intervals, and rhythm. As a music theorist, the Carmelite shows a cer-tain classicism in rooting his approach in the writings of Boethius (c. 480-524) which have strong roots in the aesthetics of proportion of the ancient Greeks (especially as associated with Pythagoras [570-495 BC] and his school).

As well as being a cathedral music director and theorist, Hothby was a composer. Only nine original works survive and were copied into the *Codex Faenza* (see below) by his fellow Carmelite, Johannes Bonadies, in the early 1470s. Scholars think most of Hothby's surviving compo-sitions were composed before he came to Lucca with the exception of his intriguingly titled *Diva panthera* (Blessed Panther); a panther ap-pears in the city arms of Lucca. *Tard'il mio cor* is in ballade form and is attractive. Hothby's *Amor* is influenced the *O rosa bella* of his fellow English composer, John Bedynham (fl. mid-1400's). Hothy's reliance on Bedynham's song is not unique: no fewer than three Masses (and many other vocal pieces) by other composers were based on the same tune. The Carmelite composer also produced two *Magnificat* settings and a setting of the *Kyrie-Christe-Kyrie* from the *Missa Cunctipotens Genitor Deus*.

Giovanni Bonadies (Godenach), O. Carm. (fl. 1450-1500)[14]

There is little information concerning origins and the life of the Carmelite musician, composer and music theorist, Johannes Bonadies. He is famous mostly on account of his work as a compiler who added significantly to the *Codex Faenza* (discussed below). Indeed sometimes the Faenza codex is referred to as the *Codex Bonadies* so synonymous is it with the work of the Carmelite. In Charles Burney's *General History of*

---

14. For the life and works of Giovanni Bonadies (Godenach), O. Carm., see "Godenach, Johannes" in *Dizionario Biografico degli Italiani*, Volume 57 (2001).

Music (London, 1780), Bonadies was cited as the teacher of Franchino Gaffùrio (1451-1522), a leading theorist of music who became director of music at the cathedral in Milan and who is by many believed to be the young man immortalised in the painting, "Portrait of a Musician" (1490), by Leonardo da Vinci (1452-1519).

Bonadies frequently signed his name upon completing the process of copying a theoretical work into the *Codex Faenza*, giving the date and sometimes his location at the time. From this we learn he was a member of the Carmelite communities at Mantua and Padua and possibly at Reggio Emilia. Bonadies also taught at the Benedictine monastery of Saint Peter in Lodi. He was active as a musician, teacher, concert organiser, conductor, and as director of music for religious services.

Just one composition is attributable to Bonadies, a *Kyrie-Christe-Kyrie* for two voices and organ which is included in the *Codex Faenza*. This work by the Carmelite composer is important since it witnesses to the emerging practice of alternating singers and solo organ (called *alternatim*) in the various parts of the Mass. In succeeding centuries the adoption of *alternatim* style of the kind envisaged by Bonadies encouraged innovation in organ building and inspired composers to write original works for the instrument (based on Mass chants), thereby adding considerably to its repertoire.

The *Codex Faenza*[15]

The *Codex Faenza* is of immense importance in the history of Western music. It is the earliest manuscript in existence which preserves purely instrumental music; it includes some music for voice in addition. Other surviving musical collections from the Middle Ages are for the most part vocal. And yet, medieval visual art abounds with representations of musicians playing instruments in both religious and secular contexts: lute, harp, fiddle, flute, organ, shawm, and often some form of percussion. Although the music is clearly instrumental, modern scholars disagree in many cases as to whether the music included in the *Codex Faenza* was intended for a keyboard instrument (e.g. the organ) or for groups of players.

Currently, the *Codex Faenza* is preserved in the Biblioteca Communale of Faenza (BC 117), near Ravenna, Italy. From the time of Bonadies until the 1860's the codex belonged to the Carmelite community at

---

15.   See the excellent notes by Michael Posch and Riccardo Delfino which accompany the CD-version of the recording of music from the *Codex Faenza* by Michael Posch with Ensemble Unicorn on the Naxos label (see list of recordings at the end of this volume for details).

Ferrara but was eventually acquired by the library at Faenza in 1889.

The *Codex Faenza* was copied between 1400 and 1420 but was added to by Bonadies in the period 1470-1474, possibly as a result of the priority given to music by the recent Mantuan Reform within the Carmelite Order and possibly under the influence of the court humanist at Mantua, Vittorino da Feltre (1378-1446).[16] For the most part, it contains arrangements for instruments of secular vocal music from Italy and France by composers such as Francesco Landini (c.1325-1397), Guillaume de Machaut (c.1300-1377), Antonio "Zacara" da Teramo (c.1350-c.1413) and Jacopo da Bologna (1340-c.1360). There are also a number of pieces based on the plainchant melody for the *Kyrie-Christe-Kyrie* from the *Missa Cunctipotens Genitor Deus* ("All-powerful God, Creator of all"), composed in the *alternatim* style, with voices and organ alternating.[17] Music by leading Carmelite composers, Bartolino da Padova and John Hothby, (both discussed above) are also represented as well as the *alternatim Kyrie* by Bonadies, previously mentioned. A number of theoretical treatises on music from the fifteenth century were added: Johannes de Muris (c.1290-c.1355), Johannes Ciconia (1370-1411) and the Carmelites, Nicasius Weyts, O. Carm., (fl. early 15th century) and John Hothby, O. Carm., are all represented in the theoretical "section" of the codex.[18]

The Carmelite Church of Saint Anna, Augsburg[19]

An important centre for music in the Carmelite Order was the Church of Saint Anna in Augsburg, Germany, which was part of a flourishing Carmelite friary founded in the early fourteenth century; the friary complex included a grammar school. The wealthy Fugger family (who had replaced the de'Medici family as the premier banking dynasty in Europe) were important local patrons in Augsburg as well as the leading financiers to the Habsburgs.

In 1508-1509, Ulrich and Jakob Fugger endowed the Carmelite church with a large chapel at its west end, designed to house their family vaults. One of the leading organists and composers of the day, the Austrian Paul Hofhaimer (1459-1537), was appointed organist

---

16. See Reinhard Strohm, *European Music 1380-1500* (Cambridge: Cambridge University Press, 1993), p. 298.

17. There is a particularly good example of this on the CD-recording of music from the *Codex Faenza* by Michael Posch with Ensemble Unicorn mentioned above.

18. Some of the theoretical topics covered in these treatises are the ars nova; counterpoint, rhythm, etc.

19. See Louise Cuyler, *The Emperor Maximilian I and Music* (London: Oxford University Press, 1973), p. 98ff. Also Strohm, *European Music*, p. 298.

(*Fugger-Organist*) of the chapel in 1518. Hofhaimer, who was already "First Organist" to the Habsburg Emperor Maximilian I, designed a new organ for the chapel which was built and installed by Jan Behaim of Dubrovnik. The instrument has two organ cases, both fitted with wing-doors which can be closed to cover the pipes. All four wing-doors (which survive today) are richly decorated, inside and out, with paintings that have interested art historians for years: the strong link with the Habsburgs achieved through the personage of the resident organist is reinforced by the depiction of a number of musicians from the imperial household.

Interestingly, in addition to the Fugger Chapel, the Church of Saint Anna includes a Chapel of the Holy Sepulchre (also constructed around 1508) which is a permanent reminder to this day of the origins of the Carmelites in the Holy Land. The chapel contains a replica of the *Anastasis*, or Rotunda, the shrine built to house Christ's tomb by the Emperor Constantine (c.272-337) in the original Church of the Holy Sepulchre in Jerusalem.

The Carmelites at Bruges[20]

That the Carmelite monastery and church at Bruges, Belgium, was a significant centre for music in the late Middle Ages and into the Renaissance is well documented. Bruges was an extremely important trading city and the Carmelite church and friary provided facilities for merchants from England and Scotland as well as from the "Hanseatic" cities of Lübeck, Hamburg and Danzig (Gdansk).[21] For example, the "Merchant Adventurers" established their headquarters at Bruges in 1344 as a confraternity of Saint Thomas Becket with its own chapel at the Carmelite church. Mass was sung there every Tuesday. A sixteenth-century document refers to a half-yearly amount being paid to the friars *"who sing in the chapel in Bruges."*[22] Carmelite music is even mentioned in connection with crime and punishment in Bruges: in 1456 the Florentine merchant, Jacopo Strozzi, who had insulted the English nation, was in recompense ordered to pay for a solemn Mass of the Holy Spirit to be celebrated (with full choral resources and organ) in the English chapel at the Carmelite church. The Scottish merchants

---

20.   See Reinhard Strohm, *Music in Late Medieval Bruges* (Oxford: Clarendon Press, 1985), pp. 63-70.

21.   The Hanseatic League (from "hanse," meaning "a convoy") was a medieval association of northern European cities, formed in 1241 and surviving until the nineteenth century. It included over one hundred cities and functioned as an independent political power.

22.   Quoted in Strohm, *Music in Late Medieval Bruges*, p. 64.

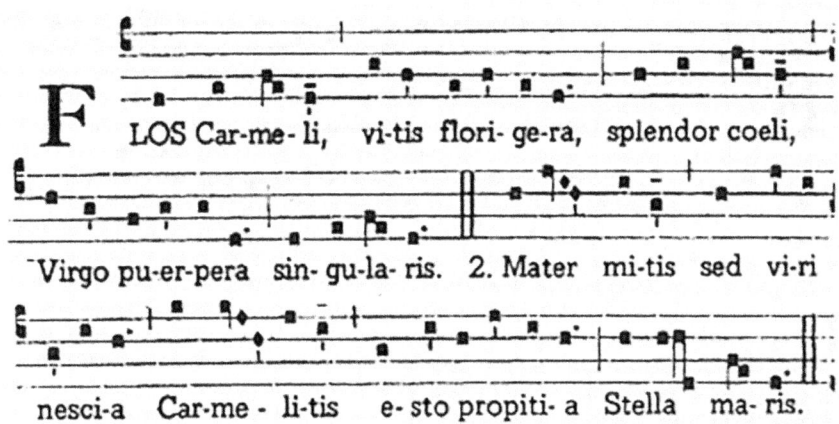

The *Flos Carmeli* is the principal hymn to Our Lady, sung in Carmelite houses. Traditionally ascribed to Saint Simon Stock, it occurs for the first time in musically notated form in a German manuscript which dates from some time after 1369. Today it is used more generally as a Marian hymn at, for example, the conclusion of the celebration of the Eucharist or the Liturgy of the Hours.

at Bruges had a chapel of Our Lady and Saint Ninian at the Carmelite church and provision was made for liturgical music (organ and choral) there.

The Carmelite convent at Bruges also provided an important gathering place for minstrels of various nationalities: to this day a nearby street bears the name *"Speelmansstrate"* (meaning "minstrel street" or, more literally, "player street").

The *Flos Carmeli* [23]

Over the centuries the *Flos Carmeli* (Flower of Carmel) has become the principal hymn to Our Lady, sung in Carmelite houses all over the world to this day. Traditionally ascribed to Saint Simon Stock, it occurs for the first time in musically notated form in a German manuscript (preserved today in the State Library of Bamberg, Germany) which dates from some time after 1369.[24] Currently, the *Flos Carmeli* is more properly sung as a sequence on the Solemnity of Our Lady of Mount

23.   See Bartolomeo Xiberta, O. Carm., "Rhythmus 'Flos Carmeli' in Liturgia Carmelitana" in *Analecta Ordinis Carmelitarum* 20 (1957), pp. 156-157.

24.   The *Flos Carmeli* also occurs in the English Carmelite missal reconstructed by Margaret Rickert in 1952: here two tiny fragments "*...endor celi virgo...*" and "*...set viri nesci...*" survive; they lack musical notation.See Margaret Ricket, *The Reconstructed Carmelite Missal: an English Manuscript of the Late XIV Century in the British Museum* (Chicago: 1952). The Bamberg manuscript contains some textual variants from the version sung today: for example, *mater puerpera* (childbearing mother) instead of *virgo puerpera* (childbearing virgin). It also has *esto propitia* ("be propitious" or "be favourable") instead of the later *da privilegia* ("grant privileges" or "grant favours") which appears in some medieval Carmelite sources.

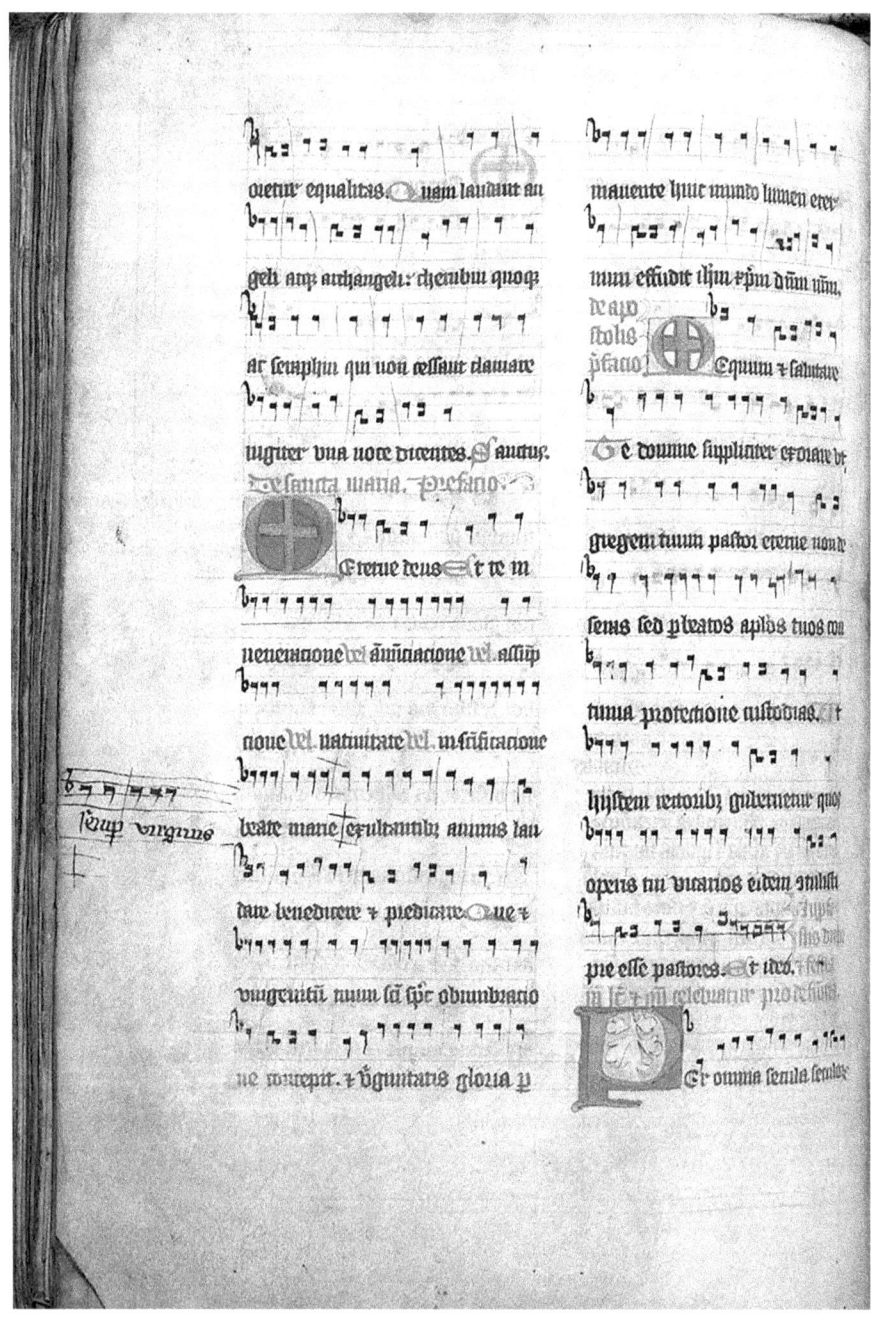

Page from the 15th century *Kilcormac Missal* (TCD MS82) an important Carmelite musico-liturgical manuscript. Between 1457 and 1458 the prior of Kilcormac commissioned Dermot O'Flanagan, a Carmelite at Loughrea friary, to produce the missal. It gives important insights into how the Carmelite liturgy was celebrated in Ireland in the fifteenth century. The document is currently housed at Trinity College, Dublin, Ireland.

Carmel, 16 July, just before the proclamation of the Gospel, but nowadays it is also used more generally as a Marian hymn at, for example, the conclusion of the celebration of the Eucharist or the Liturgy of the Hours. John Sullivan, OCD, gives the following description of this favourite Carmelite song to Mary, Mother of Carmel:

> *Flos Carmeli* is a medieval Carmelite hymn in praise of Mary, full of symbolism suited to the Holy Land origins of this Marian order. The Mother of God is described as a flower (clear allusion to the reference of Isaiah 35:1-2 to the mountain of Carmel); an ever-blossoming vine (a traditional interpretation of the name "Carmel" in the Order, though one no longer admitted by exegetes); all pure and undefiled (a possible hint at the white colour stripes alternating with the brown stripes of the hermits' mantles); and star of the sea (an obvious allusion to the location of the Carmelites' first house close to where the via maris passes by Mount Carmel).[25]

The precise origins of the current plainchant melody are somewhat obscure; the melody employed in the earliest musically notated manuscript in Bamberg is to some extent different. The tune as sung by Carmelites today betrays perhaps a certain "Eastern" quality in keeping with the Order's origins.

The Kilcormac Missal (15th Century)[26]

The historic library at Trinity College, Dublin, Ireland, contains a number of important Carmelite treasures. These include one of the oldest copies of the *Rule* of Saint Albert and also the earliest extant Carmelite liturgical document, a thirteenth-century ordinal.[27] The

---

25.   John Sullivan, OCD, "Liturgical Creativity from Edith Stein" in *Teresianum* 49 (1998), pp. 165-185. The author discusses the fascinating extra verses added to the *Flos Carmeli* by Saint Teresa Benedicta of the Cross (Edith Stein). Saint Teresa Benedicta appends several lines which dwell on the themes of the heart, of peace and of the queenship of Mary.

26.   See Patrick Mullins, O. Carm., "The Kilcormac Missal" in Salvador Ryan and Brendan Leahy, eds., *Treasures of Irish Christianity*, Vol. 2: "A People of the World" (Dublin: Veritas Publications, 2003), pp. 95-97. See also Peter O'Dwyer, O. Carm., *The Irish Carmelites* (Dublin: Carmelite Publications, 1988), pp. 64-65 and H.J. Lawlor, "The Kilcormac Missal" in *The Transactions of the Royal Irish Academy* 31 (1896-1901), pp. 393-430.

27.   Both contained in Library, Trinity College, Dublin, MS 194. See Boyce, *op. cit.*, p. 233. James Boyce, O. Carm., defines an *ordinal* as follows: "An *ordinal* is a book of rubrics that outlines the general format of a liturgy. It often includes a calendar and instructions for when to celebrate specific feasts, then lists in thorough detail all the chants and prayers to be used for the Divine Office and the Mass for the entire church year." (James Boyce, "The Ordinal of Sibert de Beka and the Development of Carmelite Liturgical Identity" in Kevin Alban, O. Carm., ed., *We Sing a Hymn of Glory to the Lord: Preparing to Celebrate Seven Hundred Years of Sibert de Beka's Ordinal 1312-2012* (Rome: Edizioni Carmelitane, 2010), p. 46). Another scholar defines an *ordinal* in simple terms as follows: "a set of summary indications as to what is said, and to some extent done, at every occasion throughout the liturgical year, with a certain amount of information as to who is supposed to do it." (Richard W. Pfaff, *The Liturgy in Medieval England* (Cambridge: Cambridge University Press, 2009), pp. 378-379).

same library also preserves an important Carmelite musico-liturgical manuscript: the *Kilcormac Missal*.[28] The Carmelite priory of Saint Mary at Kilcormac was founded by the O'Molloy family in the early fifteenth century. Between 1457 and 1458 the prior of Kilcormac, Edward O'Hacayan, commissioned his fellow Carmelite at Loughrea friary, Dermot O'Flanagan, to produce the missal. The *Kilcormac Missal* is admittedly not the finest example of medieval manuscript illumination in Ireland but it does point to an Irish Carmelite tradition of book production and musical notation. It also gives important insights into how the Carmelite liturgy was celebrated in Ireland in the fifteenth century. The *Kilcormac Missal* contains a sequence, *Mellis stilla* (A drop of honey) for the Mass of the Immaculate Conception not found elsewhere.[29] The beginning (*incipit*) of the missal and the conclusion (*colophon* or *explicit*) emphasise the links between the Irish Carmelites and the Holy Land:

> *Incipit:* "*Here begins the missal of the Brothers of the Order of Blessed Mary, Mother of God, of Mount Carmel according to the use of the Lord's Sepulchre and of the Church of Jerusalem.*"[30]

> *Explicit:* "*Here ends the missal of the Brothers of Blessed Mary of Mount Carmel extracted and taken from the approved use of the Lord's Holy Sepulchre of the Church of Jerusalem within whose bounds the said brothers have their origins. And thus the book is finished on 3 March, 1458 by Dermot O'Flanagan, brother of Loughrea, for Brother Edward O'Hacayan, Prior of the house of the Blessed Virgin Mary of Kilcormac. To whose souls may God be favourable. Amen.*"[31]

Conclusion

Having traced the broad and rich musical heritage of Carmel from the thirteenth to the early sixteenth centuries, we now turn to focus on the life and work of one of the leading Carmelite composers of the Renaissance and early modern eras, Frei Manuel Cardoso, O. Carm.

◊ ◊ ◊

---

28. Library, Trinity College, Dublin, MS 82.

29. As was noted in relation to the *Flos Carmeli* above, a sequence is a hymn sung before the proclamation of the Gospel on major feasts. For an edition of the Latin text of *Mellis stilla* and an English translation with commentary, see Patrick Mullins, O. Carm., *op. cit.*, pp. 95-97. See also Peter O'Dwyer, O. Carm., *op. cit*, pp. 64-65.

30. Lawlor, *op. cit.*, p. 396.

31. *Ibid.*

2

Frei Manuel Cardoso, O. Carm.
(c. 1566-1650)

Frei Manuel Cardoso was undoubtedly the greatest composer ever produced by the Order of Carmel. Indeed, along with his compatriots and fellow students Duarte Lôbo (c.1565-1646) and Filipe de Magalhães (c.1571-1652), he is reckoned to be one of the two most eminent Portuguese composers of all time. Frei Manuel was a leading figure in what has come to be regarded as the "golden age" of Portuguese polyphony.[1] Frequently championed by the nobility, in time he became the composer of kings, as much esteemed for his skill in choir directing as for his highly distinctive musical compositions. In his day he was the most widely published of Portuguese composers. And yet in all this Frei Manuel remained strongly conscious of his Carmelite identity, for most of his life living at the Convento do Carmo in Lisbon, where he was sub-prior. Indeed he was well regarded by his brothers in Carmel becoming definitor in 1638 and vicar provincial in 1644.

In our own time, Frei Manuel has come to be appreciated by music lovers in many countries. Several award-winning recordings of his music have appeared in recent years. In 1994 the city of Lisbon marked its designation as European City of Culture by sponsoring the production of a recording of the Carmelite composer's music, recognising in the music of Frei Manuel a worthy representative of Portugal's rich musical heritage.[2]

Several award-winning recordings of his music have appeared in recent years, with the result that the Portuguese Carmelite, his Order and the music he composed come in for frequent mention in music reviews.

---

1. See Chapter 1 for an explanation of polyphony in music.
2. See the recording by The Sixteen with Harry Christophers on the Collins Classics label detailed in the list of recordings at the end of this volume.

Life of Frei Manuel[3]

Manuel Cardoso was born at Fronteira, in the diocese of Elvas, in the year 1566. His parents were Francesco Vaz and Isabel Cardosa. At a relatively young age, Manuel was sent to study grammar and music at the seminary in Évora. There he came under the influence of Manuel Mendes (c.1547-1605) who was director of music at the cathedral; Manuel Cardoso was himself to become a choirboy at the cathedral. Another important influence at Évora was Matheo de Aranda (1495-1548) who had spent a significant amount of time in Italy and had learned from the Roman school of polyphony, presided over by the great Giovanni Pierluigi Palestrina (1525-1594). When later, in 1625, Cardoso published his *Liber primus Missarum* (First Book of Masses) he showed an intimate knowledge of Palestrina's work, basing five of his Mass settings in this volume on the work of the Roman master.

At the age of eighteen, Manuel was received into the Carmelite Order at Lisbon by the Portuguese Provincial, Simão Coelho. On 5 July 1589 Frei Manuel made his profession and was ordained priest in 1593.

It was as choir master and composer at the Carmel of Lisbon (where he was also sub-prior) that Frei Manuel began to attract the attention of royalty. For most of his life Portugal was under the jurisdiction of the Spanish crown. And so in 1631 Philip IV of Spain invited the young Carmelite composer to the court at Madrid. At that time Frei Manuel was commissioned to write a special Mass in honour of the king based on a theme suggested by the director of music at the Spanish court, Mateo Romero; in time this Mass came to be entitled the *Missa Philippina*. Cardoso's *Missa de Beata Virgine* was also dedicated to King Philip.

Frei Manuel long enjoyed the favour of João, Duke of Bragança, who in 1640 became King John IV with the restoration of the Portuguese monarchy. João was a particularly supportive patron (he kept a portrait of Cardoso in his music library), being himself a talented musician and composer.

---

3.   For the life and works of Frei Manuel Cardoso, O. Carm., see "Cardoso, Manuel" at *Grove Music Online* (www.oxfordmusiconline.com) and Prudentius Mirck, O. Carm., "Bibliotheca Carmelitana Musices" in *Carmelus* 5 (1958), pp. 100-131 (pp. 121-124 deal with Manuel Cardoso). See also the informative notes included in the CD-versions of recordings of Cardoso's music by The Sixteen and Harry Christophers, by The Tallis Scholars and Peter Phillips (notes by Peter Phillips), by the Choir of The Queen's College, Oxford and Owen Rees (notes by Owen Rees), and by the Choir of Girton College, Cambridge and Gareth Wilson (notes by Ivan Moody) (detailed in the list of recordings at the end of this volume). A significant online resource is the website of the Carmelite Choir at the Carmelite Church, Kensington, London: www.carmelitechoir.com. The choir ran a project 'Cardoso450' from 2016 to 2017 to mark the 450th anniversary of Manuel Cardoso's birth, producing a CD of previously unrecorded music by the Carmelite composer and editing a number of his works, making them more widely available to musicians.

Frei Manuel was to live at the Carmel of Lisbon for sixty-two long years. After a long illness, he passed away peacefully at the age of eighty-eight. His tomb bears the following inscription: "Here lies Father Brother Manuel Cardoso, Master and man distinguished in the art of music. Hw died on 24 November 1650."[4]

The Works of Frei Manuel

The surviving works of Frei Manuel Cardoso are those printed by Pedro Craesbeck in Lisbon in five collections, two of which were paid for by King John. Of these five collections, the first (dated 1613) is a collection of settings of the *Magnificat* and the last (dated 1648) is a general collection of motets. The other three collections (1625, 1636, and 1636) are books of Masses; the Second Book of Masses of 1636 was composed on themes provided by the Duke of Bragança. In what follows we will consider some of the highlights of Cardoso's compositional output.

Magnificat Secundi Toni (from First Book of Magnificats, 1613)

Historians of music would alert us to the fact that Frei Manuel Cardoso was a rather late representative of the art of Renaissance polyphony. Leading composers of the period tended to work to formulas, but strove to avoid the mere routine. This was particularly the case with the setting of the *Magnificat*. Indeed one could say that setting this text from Saint Luke's Gospel was the ultimate test of a composer's originality.

With his *Magnificat Secundi Toni* (Magnificat of the Second Tone),[5] Frei Manuel Cardoso finds a highly imaginative way of setting the song of Mary. Once again a hallmark of his style is his daring use of harmony. One has only to listen to the Esurientes ("He fills the starving with good things") section to hear a prolonged example of this. In the same section, Frei Manuel creates a sense of lightness and freshness (perhaps even leanness) by allowing the altos and basses to drop out altogether. This enables him to create a marvellous sense of culmination by having them return at a later stage. He even increases the number of parts towards the end of the canticle, allowing the work to come to a marvellous climax.

Frei Manuel was a member of one of the most distinctively Marian orders in the history of the Church. With his *Magnificat Secundi Toni*, he remained true to his calling as a Carmelite by producing in musical form a *Magnificat* which sounds as fresh today as when it was written.

---

4.   Mirck, *op. cit.*, p. 122.
5.   See Chapter 1 for an explanation of the system of "modes" or "tones" in medieval and Renaissance music.

Further settings of the *Magnificat* in the 1613 collection are notable and attest to the Carmelite composer's innovative skill: particularly the *Magnificat Quinti Toni* (Magnificat of the Fifth Tone) which has an eleven-note melisma (a group of notes sung to one syllable) on the word "nostros" and the *Magnificat Octavi Toni* (Magnificat of the Eighth Tone) which has a cascade of notes on the "*Sicut erat.*"[6]

Missa Miserere Mihi Domine (from First Book of Masses, 1625)

The *Missa Misere Mihi Domine* (The "Have Mercy on Me, Lord" Mass is based on a simple principle of composition known as the *cantus firmus* (literally, "a firm song"), meaning a section of melody which occurs and reoccurs and unifies the various parts of the Mass one with another. Cardoso takes his theme from an antiphon for Night Prayer (Compline) and when it occurs it does so without alteration of either text or melody. This is all very much in keeping with the instructions laid down by the Council of Trent (1545-1563) which required a plain and sober style of composition, appropriate to the liturgy and which ensured that texts remained intelligible. Cardoso's Mass setting is nonetheless highly distinctive and inventive even in following the rules. For example, he remains true to the text and melody of the cantus firmus at the "*Et incarnatus*" of the Credo and the "*Hosanna*" of the *Sanctus* but shortens the note values proportionately to great effect. The opening Kyrie is a good example of the Carmelite composer's strange but expressive use of harmony.

Requiem (from First Book of Masses, 1625)

Frei Manuel's *Requiem* was written during his time in the service of the Duke of Bragança. We do not know for whose funeral the work was composed. The Mass is in six parts, i.e. it is meant to be sung by two groups of sopranos, two groups of altos, one group of tenors, and one group of basses. While Frei Manuel's *Requiem* does show the clear influence of the Spanish composer, Tomás Luis de Victoria (1548-1611), many musicians have pointed to its original qualities.

The Carmelite composer is quite daring and unusual in his use of harmony. The very beginning of the Mass where he sets the words *Requiem aeternam dona eis, Domine* (eternal rest grant unto them, O Lord) uses intensely beautiful combinations of sound which create an ethereal effect while at the same time commanding the attention of the listener.

---

6. See the notes by Ivan Moody accompanying the CD-version of the recording of Cardoso's music by The Choir of Girton College, Cambridge and Gareth Wilson.

Similarly, in the closing *Libera me* Frei Manuel's harmony at the words *dum veneris* is so unusual that in the past some musicians presumed there was a misprint in the score. Today performers are more inclined to enjoy this particularly "spicy" (if eccentric) twist in the musical language.

In general, the *Requiem* is a good introduction to the musical world of Frei Manuel Cardoso. It combines simplicity of expression with unusual harmonies. It is also an intensely meditative and spiritual work.

Sitivit anima mea (from First Book of Masses, 1625)

The motet *Sitivit anima me*a is one of Frei Manuel Cardoso's acknowledged masterpieces. It is included in his First Book of Masses. The words are based on lines from Psalms 42 (verse 2) and Psalm 55 (verse 6): "My soul has thirsted for God who is great and ever living: when shall I come and appear before the face of my God, who will give me wings as of a dove and I shall fly and take my rest?"

Frei Manuel uses his musical skills to great effect drawing the listener deeper into the sheer poetry of the text. At the very beginning, he creates and incredible sensation of longing and pining by using some very unusual harmony around the words *sitivit anima mea* ("my soul has thirsted"). Then, later on, he evokes an unforgettable impression of flying and soaring around the words *et volabo et requiescam* (and I shall fly and take my rest).

The combination of biblical poetry with music of intense beauty in this motet can only be the fruit of a life of contemplation. One cannot help but sense the personal spirituality of the Carmelite composer. For in its own way his music is as compelling as the poetry of the better-known Saint John of the Cross.

Missa Regina Caeli (from Second Book of Masses, 1636)

The *Missa Regina Caeli* is an example of what music theorists call a "parody Mass." This means that the melodies employed by the composer are based on the melodies contained in another hymn or motet. In other words, the Mass derives its thematic material from another pre-existing source. In this case, the source is the Marian antiphon *Regina Caeli*, a chant associated with the Easter season. "Parody Masses" (as they are known) were very common in the Renaissance period. For example, Palestrina often based Masses on motets he had already written. The musical use of parody does much to stimulate the imagination of an attentive listener, helping him or her to learn to associate certain melodies with particular sacred texts.

The *Missa Regina Caeli* is a particularly joyful musical setting. This is in keeping with the Easter associations of the original Marian antiphon. Frei Manuel deliberately makes the *Et resurrexit* of the Credo sound like the *Resurrexit sicut dixit* (he has risen as he said) of the plainchant *Regina Caeli*. To the modern ear, the Mass sounds like it is in the key of F major — a key which usually conveys an airy, joyful and bright quality.

Missa Paradisi Portas (from Second Book of Masses, 1636)

By 1636, the year in which Cardoso's Second Book of Masses was published, there was considerable momentum in Portugal behind the restoration of the Portuguese monarchy in the person of João, the Duke of Bragança. One of the Mass settings included in the volume, the *Missa Paradisi Portas* (The Gates of Paradise Mass), is based on a six-part motet written by João himself. It would seem to be no coincidence that throughout the Mass Cardoso establishes a particular melodic patterns around the word *vivat*: *vivat rex* ("may the king live" or "long live the king") is a phrase often used in the acclamation of a monarch. The same *vivat* motif is also employed by the Carmelite composer in the *Benedictus* of the Mass: "Blessed is he who comes in the name of the Lord." Again, Cardoso appears to have João and the restoration of the Portuguese throne in mind here.[7]

Missa Secundi Toni (from Second Book of Masses, 1636)

The *Missa Secundi Toni* (Mass of the Second Tone) may have a rather plain title but the music is glorious. Cardoso's shows great skill both in handling multiple interweaving melodies (known as counterpoint) and in his overall economic approach to setting words to music. The final section of the Credo is a real high point.

Tulerunt lapides (from Book of Various Motets, 1648)

Tulerunt lapides (for Palm Sunday) is taken from Cardoso's last published collection of motets of 1648 and sets the words: "They took up stones to throw at Him; Jesus however concealed Himself and went out from the Temple." The Carmelite composer's characteristic rich use of

7. See the notes by Owen Rees accompanying the CD-version of the recording of Cardoso's music by The Choir of The Queen's College, Oxford and Owen Rees (detailed in the list of recordings at the end of this book).

harmony around the word *tulerunt lapides* (they took up stones) evokes the terror of the moment and his exploitation of rhythm gives a real propulsive impact to the words *ut iacerent* (to throw).

Conclusion

The music of Frei Manuel Cardoso is beautiful and intense. It is also quite distinctive and never sounds quite like the work of any other composer. The Carmelite composer seems to be at his expressive best when seeking to convey the thirsting, yearning and hunger of the human spirit. His music is often coloured by touches of dissonance which long for resolution or by restless motion which seeks to come to rest. A sense of homecoming is often achieved. Cardoso's music reflects both his keen sense of the longings of the human heart and his conviction that all comes to rest in God.

3

Benedictus of Saint Joseph (Buns), O. Carm.

Life of Benedictus of Saint Joseph [1]

Benedictus Buns was born in Geldern (near the pilgrim city of Kevelaer) in 1642. At the time of his birth, the city was part of the Spanish Netherlands; it is now in modern Germany. Little is known about Benedictus's early life before he entered the Carmelite Order at Geldern in 1659 at the age of seventeen. Benedictus made his profession of vows in 1660 and was ordained to the priesthood in 1666. Appointed to Boxmeer around 1671, he served as sub-prior to the Carmelite community there for many years. Boxmeer was located in the Province of Brabant and came under the administration of The Hague. Benedictus was the official (or "titular") organist at the Carmelite church there from 1679 until the time of his death on 6 December 1716.

That Boxmeer flourished within a Catholic enclave of the Counts van den Bergh ensured freedom of religious life and worship for the Carmelites there. The Carmelite church and monastery of Boxmeer became a centre where the arts flourished. The appointment of Benedictus ensured its already well-established musical tradition would thrive. The setting up of a Latin school at the Carmelite monastery (for the purposes of teaching the liberal arts and rhetoric) in 1658 was testament to the commitment of the friars to Catholic education; the school continued at Boxmeer until 1832. As well as having people come to them, the friars at Boxmeer also went out to the people, carrying out an extensive apostolate in Eastern Brabant, conducting missions in many places. The foundation survived both the French Revolution and secularisation to be-

---

1. For the life and works of Benedictus of Saint Joseph (Buns), O. Carm., see "Benedictus a Sancto Josepho, O. Carm." at *Grove Music Online* (www.oxfordmusiconline.com) and F.R. Noske, *Music Bridging Divided Religions* (Wilhelmshaven, 1989); the untiring work of Noske has ensured full access to the surviving works of Benedictus. See also Prudentius Mirck, O. Carm., "Bibliotheca Carmelitana Musices" in *Carmelus* 5 (1958), pp. 100-131 (pp. 121-124 deal with Manuel Cardoso). An important study in Dutch of Benedictus and his music is J.H. van der Meer, "Benedictus a Sancto Josepho van de orde der Carmeliten, 1642-1715," *Tijdschrift der Vereeniging voor Noord-Nederlands Muziekgeschiedenis*, 18/3 (1958), pp. 129-47. A valuable resource is the notes provided by Emile Wennekes for the CD-version of the recording of Benedictus's, Opus 8, *Orpheus Elianus*, by Ensemble Severin (see list of recordings at the end of this volume for details).

come the seed from which sprang modern Carmel in the Netherlands.[2]

In addition to his duties to his community as sub-prior and organist, Benedictus fulfilled the role of composer, conductor, and organist to the Van den Bergh family. He travelled to attend chapters of his Carmelite Province at Mechelen, Antwerp, and Brussels. Benedictus was also frequently consulted in the matter of organ building and restoration. During his time as organist at Boxmeer, the famous Bremser organ (two manuals and pedals) was enlarged with the addition of a third manual by Jan van Dijck in 1688. Benedictus also supervised the installation of two new organs: one in the Carmelite church at Geldern and another in the chapel of the Carmelite nuns at Boxmeer.

The Reform of Touraine

An important context for the life and music of Benedictus of Saint Joseph is the reform of Touraine. The noted Carmelite scholar, Steven Payne, introduces the reform in the following way:

> By the end of the sixteenth century, the Carmelite reform begun by Teresa of Avila had become juridically independent (as the Order of Discalced Carmelites), but in the following century, in France, a new renewal movement flowered on the ancient stock of Carmel, this time destined to remain within the original Order. Known as the reform of Touraine, this movement likewise stressed prayer, silence, and solitude, but also included a profound appreciation of the value of beautiful and well-celebrated liturgy.[3]

The origins of the reform of Touraine are to be traced back to a group of French Carmelites whose leaders, Pierre Behourt (1564-1633), Philippe Thibault (1572-1638), and later Louis Charpentier, petitioned and obtained permission from the then prior general to begin an "observant" lifestyle centred in the convent of Rennes. Here, in 1608, the community renewed their vows according to the new reform. The leading spiritual writers of the reform of Touraine were Venerable John of Saint Samson (1571-1631), Michael of Saint Augustine (1621-1685), Daniel of the Virgin Mary (1615-1678), and the tertiary, Maria Petyt (1623-1677). Major influences on the reform were the French School of Spirituality, the Flemish mystic Jan van Ruusbroec (1293-1381),

2. See Joachim Smet, O. Carm., *The Carmelites: A History of the Brothers of Our Lady of Mount Carmel*, Vol. 2: 'The Catholic Reformation 1600-1750,' Part 1, (Darien IL: Carmelite Spiritual Center, 1982) p. 292. The connection between Boxmeer and the Reform of Touraine is discussed below.

3. Steven Payne, OCD, in Steven Payne, ed., *The Carmelite Tradition* (Collegeville MN: Liturgical Press (Spirituality in History Series), 2011) p. 78. See also, Keith J. Egan, ed., *Carmelite Prayer: A Tradition for the 21st Century* (Mahwah NJ, Paulist Press, 2003) p. 56-57.

Benedictus Buns was born in Geldern in 1642 and entered the Order in 1659. Assigned to the Carmelite house in Boxmeer in 1671, he became sub-prior and served as titular organist from 1679 until his death in December 1716. Benedictus also fulfilled the role of composer, conductor, and organist to the Van den Bergh family. He frequently consulted in the matter of organ building and restoration. During his time as organist at Boxmeer, the famous Bremser organ (two manuals and pedals) was enlarged with the addition of a third manual by Jan van Dijck in 1688.

the Franciscan Hendrik Herp (c.1400-1477), Teresa of Avila, and John of the Cross.[4] As well the aforementioned emphasis on the liturgy, the reform of Touraine was strongly Marian in its outlook, it advocated a return to the "primitive Rule" of Saint Albert of Jerusalem (as mitigated by Pope Eugene IV[5]), it emphasised interior prayer, the methodical practice of meditation and examination of conscience as a community exercise, it recommended the ten-day retreat (for example, Michael of Saint Augustine proposed thirty meditations over ten days), it required the renewal of vows in the reform, it encouraged the spread of devotion to the Brown Scapular, the Forty Hours devotion, devotion to the Child Jesus, the practice of the presence of God (i.e. seeking to be recurrently "mindful" of God's presence), and aspirative prayer. Other important but less-well-known figures of the reform of Touraine were Mark of the Nativity, Mauro of the Child Jesus, and Dominic of Saint Albert.

Aspirative Prayer in the Touraine Reform

Dutch Carmelite, Sanny Bruijns, gives us the following description of the kind of aspirative prayer envisaged by the reform of Touraine:

> In the writings of Carmelite reformers like John of the Cross and John of Saint Samson, we find the prayer of aspiration. Aspiration comes from the word *"aspirare"* and this means breathing towards. This refers to inhaling the love and moving along the path that love opens up in us. It is the praying that happens in you. In a receptive soul God breathes in order to carry the soul along with him.[6]

The word "aspiration" has two senses. First, and most commonly, "aspiration" is understood in the sense of one having aspirations, aims or hopes; in this sense aspiration involves reaching out, reaching out to the future. Secondly, "aspiration" can mean the action of breathing in or

---

4. The French School of Spirituality (École Française) included Cardinal Philippe de Bérulle (1575-1629), Jean-Jacques Olier (1608-1657), Saint Jean Eudes (1601-1680), and Madame Acarie (Mother of the Incarnation, OCD) (1566-1618); Philippe Thibault, O. Carm., was associated with the circle of Madame Acarie. Saint Francis de Sales was an important influence.

5. It is customary to identify three phases in the development of the Rule of Carmel. The first ("Albertina") was that drawn up by Saint Albert of Jerusalem at the beginning of the thirteenth century. The second phase ("Innocentiana") coincides with the first major mitigations of Albert's Rule, which were the result of the petitioning of Pope Innocent IV by the Carmelites (who requested that "he deign to clarify and correct certain doubts and mitigate certain severities"), and which were approved by the bull *Quae honorem* (September 12, 1247). The third phase ("Eugeniana") came with the mitigations approved by Pope Eugene IV with the bull *Romani Pontificis* (February 15, 1432) which permitted the Carmelites to eat meat three days a week, and to walk about their churches, cloisters and grounds at certain times, thus not having to remain continually in their cells. At various times in the history of the Carmelite Order there was a variety of views as to what constituted the "primitive rule": for example, Saint Teresa of Avila considered the *Rule* as mitigated by Pope Innocent to be primitive.

6. Sanny Bruijns, "The Carmelite Way of Prayer," *Carmel in the World*, 53, 3 (2014), pp. 231-234, p. 234.

breathing out: the action or process of drawing breath or else the action of pronouncing a sound with an exhalation of breath. Aspirative prayers are short prayers. Common examples in the Catholic tradition would be "Sacred Heart of Jesus, have mercy on me" or "Come, Holy Spirit." An example from the Christian East is the Jesus Prayer: "Lord, Jesus Christ, Son of God, have mercy on me a sinner." An aspiration may even be a simple (and breathy) "ah" or "oh."[7] The key thing for John of Saint Samson is that prayer of aspiration is possible only because God already loves us and wants us to live totally in the space of his love. Our aspirations are never in vain since they begin and end in God. Furthermore, they are as natural as breathing in and breathing out and enable us to unite our daily routine with God. John says:

> Thus holiness does not consist in feeling or not feeling God in his emanations or radiations or the soul being touched with his divine emanations, but in true and essential love that is practical and makes everything being done in God.[8]

And writing about those who practice the prayer of aspiration, John says:

> It happens that these persons are in themselves and are not at all carried outside themselves through powerful and extraordinary attraction of God. Their usual activity is then being carried in God, full of love, ardent and essential, as much as is possible for them. It is for them as easy as breathing in and out. They do it almost as often because of their habituation to this.[9]

The Prophet Elijah in the Touraine Reform

Even a cursory glance at the works of Benedictus of Saint Joseph are revealing of the central place given to the two patrons of Carmel, Elijah and Mary, in his musical output. Elijah requires particular comment given the context of the times in which Benedictus composed. The Elijan dimension of the Order's identity was strongly emphasised by leading figures in the reform of Touraine, such as Michael of Saint Augustine and Daniel of the Virgin Mary. This came in the face of increasing attacks

---

7.   Sanny Bruijns writes: "Aspirations are short and quick prayers of heaving sighs. The sighing of the soul, which utters an 'oh' or an 'ah' is like the prayer of someone who does not know how to pray. It is like the Spirit, who comes to rescue us in weakness and pleads with unspeakable sighs. In his letter to the Romans, Saint Paul speaks about his hope for the coming glory. With Saint Paul, Carmelites live from hope. Our praying is like the coming of the Messiah. Our working in silence is carried by the hope which lives in our heart. But *because our hope is directed towards the invisible, our waiting and expecting must be accompanied with perseverance.*" (Bruijns, *op. cit.*, p. 234).

8.   Quoted in Falco Thuis, O. Carm., "Venerable John of Saint Samson 1571-1636" in *Carmel in the World*, 56, 2 (2017), pp. 133-142, p. 139.

9.   *Ibid.*, 139.

from the Bollandists who cast doubt on the Elijan succession. This was largely initiated by the Flemish Jesuit scholar and revisionist hagiographer, Daniel Papebroch (1628-1714), in 1668 and the ensuing (at times, disedifying) debate was to last for thirty years until the Holy See enjoined silence in 1698 on both sides. At the risk of overstating the point, it can be asserted that the publication of music by Benedictus with its strong Elijan emphasis served to bolster the Carmelite position at a time when the Order felt under attack. All his *opus* numbers appeared in the period 1666-1700, and it is difficult to resist the temptation to speculate that the appearance in 1699 of Benedictus's *Orpheus Elianus* (The Elijan Orpheus) would have had a special resonance. In 1727, eleven years after Benedictus's death, the famous statue of Elijah by Agostino Cornacchini (1686-1764) was installed in Rome's Saint Peter's Basilica as one of the four great founders of religious orders.[10]

Setting aside the polemic and occasional triumphalism, it is important to note the profound way in which writers in the reform of Touraine such as Daniel of the Virgin Mary and especially Michael of Saint Augustine engaged in deep reflection on the role of Elijah in the spiritual life of Carmel.[11] With them, a Carmelite's being a successor of Elijah is far less an exterior matter than a call to profound interiority. The Carmelite scholar, Christopher O'Donnell, differentiates between considering Elijah in terms of historical and spiritual succession:

> Today Carmelites would not see their Order going back in an historical line to the prophet who flourished more than 800 years before Christ. But there are spiritual links. The first Carmelites venerated the prophet, and established themselves near the fountain called Elijah's on Mount Carmel. Moreover they saw their life as in spiritual succession to that of the prophet.[12]

When in 1670 Daniel of the Virgin Mary publishes his *Phoenix of the World, Miracle of Grace and Nature, Saint Elijah the Prophet, Princeps of Monastic Religion Life, Patriarch of the Carmelite Order,* he steers clear for the major part from the issue of succession, preferring to emphasise the biblical figure of Elijah, Elijah as understood within the Christian tradition and Elijah as perfect mirror of the virtues of poverty, chastity, and

---

10.   The inscription at the base of the statue reads: "*Universus Carmelitarum Ordo fundatori suo Sancto Eliae Prophetae erexit a MDCCXXVII*" (The whole Carmelite Order has erected this [statue] to its founder Saint Elijah the Prophet).

11.   See Jane Ackerman, *Elijah: Prophet of Carmel* (Washington DC: ICS Publications, 2002), pp. 227-228. Michael of Saint Augustine develops a highly intricate philosophical, moral and theological argument which attempts to bring together both the Rule of Albert and the Elijan succession. The detail is beyond the scope of this discussion.

12.   Christopher O'Donnell, O. Carm., in The Irish Province of Carmelites, *Meeting God: Carmelite Reflections and Prayers* (Dublin: Columba, 2007), p.19.

obedience. Daniel tells how Elijah dedicated himself daily to vocal and mental prayer, psalmody, meditation, flight from the world, as well as the virtues of prudence, justice, fortitude, temperance, faith, charity, and zeal.[13] Many years later, Blessed Titus Brandsma continued to emphasise the importance of interior, spiritual succession from the Prophet Elijah, speaking of living in the "spirit and strength of Elijah" and stating that "the life of Elijah is the shortest summary of the Order's life"[14]

Benedictus of Saint Joseph, Boxmeer and the Reform of Touraine

Both Daniel of the Virgin Mary and Michael of Saint Augustine were responsible for the Carmelite foundation at Boxmeer in 1652, the community to which Benedictus Buns was appointed around 1671. His taking of the double name "Benedictus of Saint Joseph" itself reflects the practice within the reform of Touraine and his dedication to music and liturgy, together with his obvious devotion to Elijah, Mary, and the Eucharist, resonates with its core values. No simple equation can be made between music and the prayer of aspiration but so much of music is about breath and phrasing. It is perhaps not far-fetched to suggest Benedict would consider composer, player, singer, and listener all find their place together in that space of loving encounter between human and divine. It is often said that music opens up onto the transcendent. It might be argued that in the Carmelite tradition music when composed, played, sung, and heard may be seen to open onto divine love, which is an altogether warmer idea.

Works of Benedictus of Saint Joseph[15]

The works of Benedictus of Saint Joseph are for the most part well preserved. It is customary for the works of a composer (both single pieces and pieces grouped together) to be given an "*opus*" (i.e. "work") number. Of the nine opus numbers produced by Benedictus of Saint Joseph, seven survive in their entirety to this day.

Exceptionally, being a collection of thirteen instrumental church sonatas, Opus 8 is entirely instrumental. The other volumes published by Benedictus are for the most part collections of liturgical music, for one or several voices, with instrumental accompaniment; occasionally an in-

---

13. See Ackerman, *op. cit*, p. 229-230.
14. Titus Brandsma, O. Carm., *The Beauty of Carmel* (Dublin: Clonmore and Reynolds, 1955), p. 26.
15. The most complete list of the works of Benedictus a Sancto Josepho (Buns) is to be found in Van der Meer, *op. cit.*

strumental piece is included (e.g. at the end of Opus 5 which concludes with a *sonata finalis*). The several tomes of the Carmelite's compositional corpus include multiple Mass settings (including two *Requiem* Masses), Marian antiphons, always a *Salve Regina* [one in each volume] and sometimes a *Laurentian Litany* [Litany of Loreto], *Regina Caeli* or *Ave Regina Caelorum*, a *Te Deum*, Eucharistic hymns (several settings of *Tantum Ergo*), dialogues and other spiritual texts set to music.

The following are the nine surviving opus numbers by Benedictus of Saint Joseph (with publisher, location and year of publication in each case).[16]

> Opus 1- *Missae, Litaniae et Motetta*, Petrus Phalasius, Antwerp 1666
>
> Opus 2 - *Corona Stellarum Duodecim* (Crown of Twelve Stars, cf. *Revelation* 12:1), Petrus Phalasius, Antwerp 1673
>
> Opus 3 - *Flosculi Musici*, Petrus Phalasius, Antwerp 1672
>
> Opus 4 - *Musica Montana in Monte Carmelo Composita*, Lucas de Potter, Antwerp 1677
>
> Opus 5 - *Completoriale Melos Musicum*, Lucas de Potter, Antwerp 1678
>
> Opus 6 - *Encomia sacra musice decantanda*, Arnold van Eynden, Utrecht 1683
>
> Opus 7 - *Orpheus gaudens ac lugens sive Cantica gaudii ac luctus*, Hendrik Aertssens, Antwerp, 1693
>
> Opus 8 - *Orpheus Elianus è Carmelo in orbem editus*, Estienne Roger, Amsterdam 1699
>
> Opus 9 - *Missa sacris ornata canticis*, Estienne Roger, Amsterdam c1699-1700

In addition, Benedictus of Saint Joseph compiled and edited two major collections of plainchant, supplying his own technical and theoretical notes: *A Processionale juxta usum Fratrum Beatae Virginae Mariae de Monte Carmelo* (Antwerp, 1711) and a *Manuale Chori ad usum Fratrum Beatae Virginae Mariae de Monte Carmelo* (Brussels, 1721). Both volumes were intended (as their names suggest) for use in the liturgical celebrations of Carmelite communities on a day-to-day basis, reflecting the emphasis on liturgy and on liturgical spirituality encouraged by the reform of Touraine.

16. The contents of each of these is given in detail by Van der Meer, *op. cit.*

Compositional Style of Benedictus of Saint Joseph

Stylistically the music of Benedictus of Saint Joseph is Baroque and is strongly influenced by the same kind of aesthetic evident in the work of Italian composers such as Claudio Monteverdi (1567-1643) and Arcangelo Corelli (1653-1713). Affinities also exist between the music of Benedictus and that of his contemporary, the French composer Marc-Antoine Charpentier (1643-1704), who was himself strongly influenced by the Italian school.

Paying just a little attention to the theory and practice of Monteverdi helps us gain an insight into the Carmelite composer's style.[17] In 1605 Monteverdi adopted the terms *prima prattica* and *seconda prattica* (first practice and second practice). *Prima prattica* referred to the older music of composers such as Giovanni Pierluigi da Palestrina (1525-1594).[18] In this first practice, music dominates the text, at least according to Monteverdi. *Seconda prattica* applied to the newer music of Monteverdi's time (including his own) where the text dominated the music. Apart from an emphasis on text, there were three further characterisitcs of the newer *seconda prattica*. First, there is an emphasis on solo voice (*monody*) accompanied by an instrument or group of instruments. Secondly, composers often provided this bass line (often played by a cello or lute) with "figures" (or "numbers") which indicated to the other players (often an organist or harpsichordist) how to "fill in" the harmony: hence the increasing importance of what came to be called *figured bass*. The instrument playing the bass line and the instruments filling in the harmony were together known as the *basso continuo* which would often be the core of larger orchestras. Thirdly, what is known as *concertato* style emerged as part of the *seconda prattica* which involved contrast between high and low, soft and loud, between basso continuo and full orchestra, between solo voice and chorus or between solo instrument and orchestra.

These three features of the new (what Monteverdi called "*seconda prattica*") are all readily recognisable hallmarks of the compositional style of Benedictus of Saint Joseph, who delighted in exploiting the potential for contrast offered by *concertato* technique.

Musical Highlights

(see the explanations above of *basso continuo* and *concertato*)

---

17.   For an excellent and accessible introduction to the Baroque style in composition see Edward Schaefer, *Catholic Music through the Ages: Balancing the Needs of a Worshipping Church* (Chicago: Hillenbrand Books, 2008), pp. 90-95.

18.   One could also take the polyphonic compositional style of the Carmelite composer, Frei Manuel Cardoso, O. Carm., as an example here. See Chapter 2.

Salve Regina (Opus 1, no. 3)

We noted earlier that Benedictus of Saint Joseph includes a setting of the *Salve Regina* (Hail, Holy Queen) in each of his published volumes. The setting from Opus 1 is elaborate in that it is composed for two sopranos, alto, tenor, and bass, a full chorus (soprano, alto, tenor, and bass), two violins, bassoon, and basso continuo. Benedictus follows the text of the Marian antiphon closely and the large forces are used very expressively.

Magnificat (Opus 5, no. 3)

The setting of the song of Mary, the *Magnificat*, from Benedictus's Opus 5 is compact and simple in its expression. It is scored for soprano, tenor, and bass, a full chorus (soprano, alto, tenor, and bass), two violins, bassoon, and basso continuo. In typical *concertato* style, it alternates between full ensemble and one to three soloists. After a slow opening with a gently swaying, yet stately, rhythm, the full chorus sing *Magnificat anima mea Dominum* (My soul glorifies the Lord.) This is followed by a fast passage of sheer joy where the full choir sings *Et exultavit spiritus meus in Deo Salutari meo* (my spirit rejoices in God, my Saviour). Thereafter the music alternates between slow and fast, and parts of Mary's song are shared out between solo voices, soloists singing together, and the full chorus. *Fecit potentiam in brachio suo* (He puts forth his arm in strength) is vigorously sung by a solo tenor. The Carmelite composer employs a powerful, pounding rhythm to accompany the words *deposuit potentes de sede* (he casts the mighty from their thrones). Benedictus sets the words *Suscepit Israel puerum suum: recordatus misericordiae suae* (He protects Israel, his servant, mindful of his mercy) very tenderly, allowing the chorus some very lightly accompanied moments so the human voices can be heard more clearly singing in harmony. The whole *Magnificat* setting ends in jubilation: the opening stately rhythm is recalled for the *Gloria patri* (Glory be) and at *sicut erat in principio* (as it was in the beginning) the music takes flight, allowing the words to ring out, until the final *Amen* is reached.

Posita in media (Opus 5, no. 5)

Posita in media is a dialogue between the Soul, the Devil, the Flesh, and the World and is set for soprano, alto, tenor, and bass soloists, two violins, viola da gamba, and basso continuo. Dialogue is itself an ancient

form. Benedictus and his contemporaries had a liking for it, especially
in the religious context. Musical dialogues of the kind composed by the
Carmelite began to emerge around 1600.[19] They usually did not set liturgical texts but could nonetheless be used at a suitable point in the celebration of the Mass or the Liturgy of the Hours. They were considered
to have an educational role. Dialogue, with its inbuilt diversity of voices
and characters, lends itself particularly to being set to music in the *concertato* (i.e. contrasting) style. In his Opus 3, Benedictus sets a dialogue
between Christ and Mary Magdalene, *Mulier, quid ploras?* (Woman, why
do you cry?). In his Opus 6 Benedictus composes music for no fewer
than four dialogues: a dialogue between a blessed and damned person; a
dialogue between God and two (male) sinners; a dialogue between God
and two (female) sinners; a dialogue between Christ, Mary Magdalene,
and Martha. The Opus 5 dialogue is quite dramatic (operatic even) with
the poor human soul beset from all sides, being offered empty promises,
by the World, the Flesh, and the Devil, sometimes singly, sometimes
together. The Devil (sung by a bass) sounds particularly terrifying. A
vocal battle ensues (with the orchestra providing furious music) with
the soul, drawing herself up to her full strength and taking up spiritual
weapons, in the music literally hurling the word "arms" (*arma, arma!*)
at her enemies who try to sue for peace (*pax, pax!*) only to be banished
to Hell. In the end the soul triumphs: "Hurrah! The lion of the race of
Judah has triumphed. Blow up the trumpet in the New Moon... And I
rise triumphing into heaven." As for the World, the Flesh, and the Devil:
"Alas, we fall tumbling into Hell."[20] Benedictus of Saint Joseph may be
seen to have been a major exponent of the 17th century dialogue genre,
a musical genre which has only recently come to be rediscovered and appreciated by music scholars.[21]

Domine, Ne in furore (Opus 6, no. 7)

Domine, Ne in furore is written for a deep bass soloist, two violins, viola
da gamba, and basso continuo. Here Benedictus reminds one of some of
the arias for bass in the oratorio, *Messiah*, by the later composer George
Frederick Handel (see Chapter 4). In typical Baroque musical form, the
music often takes its lead from the words and at key points engages in an
amount of word painting (i.e. the music reflects the literal meaning of

---

19. See the excellent accompanying notes to the CD-version of *Saints and Sinners: 17th-Century
Musical Dialogues* (for details see the list of recordings at the end of the book).
20. See translation of the text provided in the notes to the CD-version of *Saints and Sinners, op.
cit.*, pp. 23-26.
21. In large part due to the work of the musicologist and leading scholar of Benedictus of Saint
Joseph, Frits Noske, who is mentioned above.

the words), e.g. the words *in furore* (in anger) and *miserere* (have mercy). This is *concertato* style at its best with the Carmelite composer contrasting slow and fast, loud and soft, light and shade, soloist and orchestra to great effect. Benedictus begins the work with a particularly beautiful extended instrumental prelude.

O sors optata (Opus 6, no. 9)

The lengthy motet, *O sors optata*, from his Opus 6 is scored for two sopranos, two violins, bassoon, and basso continuo. Benedictus sets a contemporary devotional text. The two sopranos rival the two violins in virtuosity. Calm and contemplative passages in duple time alternate with sections in triple time which employ a variety of dance rhythms: a sarabande (a stately Spanish dance) accompanies the words *In Te est gaudium* (In You is joy) and a chaconne (a repeated bass dance) partners the words *Torrente voluptatis tuae* (the torrent of Your grace).

Obstupescite (Opus 6, no. 12)[22]

The opening word says it all *Obstupescite* (think of "stupefied" or "stupefaction" in English): "Be amazed, o heavens, at these tidings, and rejoice greatly, o ye gates, for the Lord in his greatness has so done unto us" are set to robust music for bass soloist with incisive use of rhythm. This is followed by a gentler section for soprano solo: "Who love the Lord and fear Him: Come, and I shall tell you what great things He has done unto my soul: He led me into his wine-cellar, He gave witness of his great love for me." This leads to a lively duet between bass and soprano which becomes particularly poignant at the words *Dominus Jesus pro me et non pro vobis mortuus est* (Lord Jesus died for me but not for you).

Orpheus Elianus (Opus 8, no. 1-13)

Orpheus was the poet of Greek mythology who could enchant through the beauty of his singing and his playing of the lyre. He was a kind of icon of musical inspiration for composers and artists of Benedictus's day. Orpheus is also named in the title of the Carmelite composer's Opus 7 *Orpheus Gaudens ac Lugens* (Orpheus Rejoicing and Weeping). With his Opus 8, *Orpheus Elianus*, Benedictus is drawing musical inspiration from Elijah, prophet of Carmel and spiritual inspiration of Carmelites. Just as the Orpheus of Greek mythology could beguile with the beauty

22. *Ibid.*, pp. 26-27.

of his music making, Benedictus is keen, it would seem, to see the potential in music for expressing joy and sorrow and for drawing the listener to contemplation of higher things. The volume contains thirteen instrumental church sonatas and is dedicated to Oswald van den Bergh and his wife (Oswald was the son of Albert, the founder of Boxmeer monastery). *Orpheus Elianus* is scored for two violins, viola da gamba, and basso continuo. All thirteen pieces alternate between slow and fast sections and employ often stirring melodies. Several dance rhythms are employed: e.g. minuet, jig, and gavotte. Benedictus very cleverly arranges the sonatas (each of which is in a different key) according to the Circle of Fifths, with minor keys first and major ones following.[23] As a master stroke, the Carmelite composer achieves the shift from minor to major in the seventh piece (moving from F-sharp minor into E-flat major).

Ave Maria (Opus 9)

This exquisite setting of the *Ave Maria* (Hail Mary) begins with the plainchant tune and continues as a duet between two singers. For its haunting simplicity this work is one of the finest compositions set down by Benedictus of Saint Joseph.

Conclusion

Benedictus of Saint Joseph (Buns) is one of the greatest composers the Carmelite Order has produced. He was certainly Carmel's most significant composer of the Baroque era in classical music. His life and work deserve to be better known. His music is a constantly inspiring, with its skilful marrying of text and music. Both the music and the life of Benedictus of Saint Joseph are also important windows onto movements in Carmelite history and spirituality which would continue to influence the Order well beyond seventeenth-century Europe.

---

23.   The Circle of Fifths is a way of showing in the form of a diagram the relationship between different keys in Western music. It is usually shown as a circle with the names of keys around it. If you take any key in the circle, its fifth is the one to its right.It is useful in music theory but also practically, having the circle of fifths in mind, helps a musician to move between different keys (known as modulation).

4

George Frederick Handel's Music for the Carmelites[1]

The feast of Our Lady of Mount Carmel was a major event in 18th-century Rome. Just inside the northern limits of the city, in Piazza del Popolo, the Carmelite church of Santa Maria in Montesanto became the annual focus for lavish festivities, with illuminated arches being erected in the surrounding streets stretching as far as Piazza di Spagna and Piazza San Carlo. This festival in honour of the principal patron of the Carmelite Order was not only visually stunning. Each year worshippers at the church were also treated to a veritable musical extravaganza provided by some of the most celebrated Italian composers of the day.

In January 1707 something different happened. A foreigner of extraordinary musical ability made his mark in Rome. The diarist Francesco Valesio tells us: "A German has arrived here in Rome, an excellent harpsichordist and composer. Today he showed his skill, playing the organ at the church of Saint John [Lateran] to universal admiration."[2] This young German (he was twenty-two) was none other George Frederick Handel. Handel was soon to win the favour of a number of important patrons including the Marquis Francesco Ruspoli and Cardinal Carlo Colonna. The Colonna family had long been patrons of the Carmelite Order and it was through them that the young Handel was commissioned to provide music for the celebration of the Feast of Our Lady of Mount Carmel in July 1707.

In recent years the importance of the music Handel composed during his time in Italy has come to be more and more appreciated. Indeed, some music he composed in this period was eventually to reappear in later works better known to listeners today.'

---

1. The most important studies concerning Handel's music for the Carmelites are by Graham Dixon: Graham Dixon, "Handel's Music for the Carmelites: A Study in Liturgy and Some Observations on Performance" in *Early Music* 15 (1987), pp. 16-29 and "Handel's Music for the Carmelites: A Study in Liturgy and Some Observations on the Performance of the Music" in *Carmelus* 34 (1987), pp. 78-93. See also Dixon's notes to the CD-version of Handel's music for the Carmelites conducted by Marc Minkowski (details in the list of recordings at the end of this volume). Dixon reconstructed second Vespers for the Feast of Our Lady of Mount Carmel for a broadcast on BBC radio and other networks in 1985, attracting much international attention at the time. The broadcast performance took place in the original Roman church of Santa Maria in Montesanto.
2. Quoted in Dixon's notes (p. 6) to the Minkowski recording mentioned above.

Life of Handel[3]

The family of Handel was of Silesian origin. Georg, the composer's father, was an important medical doctor in Halle and at the court of Saxe-Weissenfels. He married for the second time when he was already over sixty and his second son by this marriage, George Frederick, was born in 1685.

George Frederick showed extraordinary musical ability from a very early age. His father, for his part, did everything to discourage his son from following a career in music, preferring that he would study law. However, on one occasion, when he was only seven, George Frederick accompanied his father on a visit to the court at Weissenfels and so astonished the duke and his musical director with his organ playing that he was promptly sent for musical training under Friedrich Wilhelm Zachow in Halle.

Even though his father died in 1697, Handel decided to pursue legal studies and entered the university of Halle in February 1702. In March of the same year he was appointed temporary organist at the cathedral there. The following year Handel decided to give up his legal studies and to go to Hamburg to build up his musical career. There he worked as a violinist in the opera orchestra and wrote two German operas which were very successful. In 1706 he decided to seek his fame and fortune in Italy.

Handel produced his opera *Rodrigo* at Florence in 1706 and visited Rome, Naples and Venice. He did all he could to visit music academies and to meet notable Italian composers, seeking to learn from the Italian school of composition.

After the huge success of his opera *Agrippina* in Venice in 1709, Handel decided to accept the position of *Kapellmeister* (music director) at the court of Hanover. However, almost immediately he sought leave to go to London. From this point on Handel was associated with England and the English court, producing such famous works as the *Water Music*, *Music for the Royal Fireworks*, operas such as *Rinaldo* and oratorios such as *Messiah, Esther, Deborah, Solomon* and *Judas Maccabeus*. In 1727 Handel produced a set anthems for the coronation of George II. For the rest of his life England was his home. On 6 April 1759, he played the harpsichord for a performance of *Messiah*. Returning home that night he felt unwell and took to bed saying: "I wish I may die on Good Friday, in the hope of meeting my dear Lord and Saviour on the day of His

---

3.   For the life and works of George Frederick Handel, see Donald Burrows, *Handel*, 2nd edition (Oxford: Oxford University Press (Master Musicians Series), 2010).

Born in 1685, George Frederick Handel, showed extraordinary musical ability from a very early age. When he was only seven, George Frederick accompanied his father on a visit to the court at Weissenfels and so astonished the duke and his musical director with his organ playing that he was promptly sent for musical training under Friedrich Wilhelm Zachow in Halle. When he died in 1759, he was recognized for his great contribution to music.

Resurrection."[4] George Frederick Handel died on Saturday 14 April and was laid to rest in Westminster Abbey. Several years later the great composer Ludwig van Beethoven was asked who was the greatest composer of all time. "Handel," he answered "because he achieved the greatest effect with the simplest of means."[5] Handel was indeed an extraordinarily

4.   Quoted in Geoffrey Hindley, ed.,*The Larousse Encyclopedia of Music* (Secaucus NJ: Chartwell Books, 1971), p. 216.

5.   Beethoven's views on Handel were reported by the Austrian composer Ignaz Seyfried. See Ignaz Seyfried, ed., *Louis [sic] van Beethoven's Studies*, transl. Henry Hugh Pierson (Leipzig, Hamburg and

talented composer with an extraordinary gift for combining rhythm and melody in works which have stood the test of time. His *Messiah* is performed by thousands of music groups all over the world to this day. In recent years people are rediscovering his early work, especially the music he composed during his Italian sojourn. Above all, musicians and music enthusiasts have begun to appreciate the extraordinary beauty of the liturgical music he wrote as a young man for the Carmelite Order.

The Carmelite Church of Santa Maria in Montesanto

Before we consider Handel's music for the Carmelites in more detail it is worthwhile considering the location in which the work was originally performed. The church of Santa Maria in Montesanto derives its title from the principal convent of a reform movement which thrived within the Carmelite Order in Italy in the 17th and 18th centuries. Inspired by friars such as Desiderio Placa and the Prior General, Henry Sylvio, a group of Carmelites sought to reform their way of life by living a stricter observance in keeping with the "primitive rule" of the Order (the rule of Saint Albert as mitigated by Pope Innocent IV). The main emphasis of the new reform was the necessity of prayer in solitude. Broadly speaking the reformers sought to emulate the Discalced Carmelite reform while remaining part of the Order as a whole.

In the middle of the 17th century the friars of the reform of Monte Santo sought to expand their presence in Rome. Pope Alexander VII wished to erect two churches flanking the Via del Corso at the point where it joins Piazza del Popolo. The twin churches of Our Lady of Montesanto and Our Lady of the Miracles were the result of his plan. The first of these was to become the principal Roman church of the Carmelite Monte Santo reform. Its foundation stone was laid in 1662. Piazza del Popolo with its twin churches is a major attraction for visitors to Rome to this day.

The Liturgy for the Feast of Our Lady of Mount Carmel

The principal liturgical celebrations for the feast of Our Lady of Mount Carmel are first Vespers (celebrated the evening before), the Mass and second Vespers (on the evening of the feast). The Carmelite rite required the singing of five psalms at Vespers as well as numerous antiphons, responses, hymns, and canticles.

Much of the liturgy of Vespers was chanted using simple tones, but it

---

New York: Schuberth and Company, 1853), p. 16.

The church of Santa Maria in Montesanto in Rome, the center of the Monte Santo reform of the Carmelite Order during the 17th and 18th centuries. Handel's music for the Carmelites was performed there for the Feast of Our Lady of Mount Carmel in 1707.

had become customary for the Carmelites at S. Maria in Montesanto to commission composers (with the help of patronage) to write lavish settings of the Latin psalms and antiphons for soloists, choir, and orchestra. In response to such a commission the young Handel set about composing music for the feast of Our Lady of Mount Carmel on 16 July 1707.

It is important to realise that Handel's music for the Carmelites is not a single unified work like an opera or *oratorio* (such as *Messiah*). In fact Handel was concerned with the business of writing a number of separate psalm settings, motets, and antiphons which were to be inserted into the Carmelite liturgy at the appropriate points. Much of the ordinary chanting at Vespers and Mass would be undertaken by the Carmelite friars with the choir and soloists singing the more elaborate settings.

There has been some debate among scholars as to whether Handel's music was intended for first or second Vespers or for Mass. Some have even questioned whether the music was written for the Carmelite feast at all! However, the evidence provided by the latest scholarship points towards the conclusion that Handel did indeed write music for the celebration of the feast of Our Lady of Mount Carmel in 1707 and that his psalm and antiphon settings were intended (along with music by other composers) to be spread out between the various liturgies.

Scholars have been greatly aided in their work by the discovery in 1985 of a number of Handel's musical scores in Manchester, England. We now know that Handel was working under much pressure at the beginning of July 1707. He was obviously working to complete his music before 16 July and the celebration of the Carmelite feast. For example, the *Laudate pueri* was completed on 8 July, and the manuscript of *Nisi Dominus* bears the date 13 July. Like many composers of his day Handel certainly knew what it was to work to a deadline!

Saeviat tellus

From a purely Carmelite point of view the most interesting text set to music by Handel is the motet *Saeviat tellus* for solo soprano. It could have been sung either at first or second Vespers or during Mass. This motet exhorts the Carmelite Order to remain fearless in the face of all adversity, relying as it does on the protection of the Virgin Mary. The text tells of the appearance of Our Lady to Pope Honorius III, encouraging him to give official recognition to the Carmelite Order in 1226.

Handel's music for this Carmelite motet is extremely dramatic and sounds very much like a battle cry. Indeed this setting has much in common with the kind of battle arias Handel was later to write for his operas and oratorios. One cannot help but marvel at the assurance with which the young German composer writes, and the sensitivity with which he sets the Latin text. In the opening section the Carmelites are reminded that "though Lucifer roars among the flames with deceptions and cunning, you may laugh at the threats of Hell."

In the middle section Handel writes an exquisitely gentle setting of the words "O Sweet night, serene peace, remain long and unchanging for the Carmelites." To the background of sweet and soothing music the soprano sings to reassure the Order of the caring protection of Mary (*lux amabilis Mariae*).

In the following sections the heavens are addressed: "faithful stars, you are charged with saving the Carmelites from the world." The rder is exhorted to be "victorious" (*Carmelitae triumphatae*) under the protection of Mary (*sub tantae Virginis tutela*) and to "rejoice" (*Carmelitae jubilate*). The motet ends with a rousing *Alleluia*.

Scholars have pointed out how many of the melodies employed by Handel in this Carmelite motet find their way into his later better-known works.

Salve Regina

Another impressive setting by Handel is his *Salve regina* for soprano and small orchestra. It would seem that Handel composed this work at the Ruspoli country seat of Vignanello in June 1707, and perhaps it was not originally intended for the Carmelite liturgy. However, it seems likely that Handel did indeed reuse this setting on July 16th for the Carmelite feast. According to the Carmelite *Caeremoniale* of 1616 Vespers on feasts of Our Lady was concluded with a procession to the altar of Our Lady, during which the *Salve Regina* was sung.

The first two sections of Handel's setting of the *Salve Regina* ("Hail, Queen of heaven" and "To Thee do we cry.") are very intimate and perhaps even a little sad in tone. However, this is followed by a bubbly third section with an extremely impressive part for the organ. Handel probably played this himself. It is certainly designed to impress!

Dixit Dominus

Handel's setting of the *Dixit Dominus* (Psalm 109) was possibly originally composed for an occasion other than the feast of Our Lady of

Mount Carmel. However, it fits in very well as the first of five psalms at second Vespers. Here Handel writes for full choir, two sopranos, alto, two tenors, and bass. The work is quite grandiose and would certainly have made a great impression at the beginning of Vespers. Once again, Handel sets the Latin text in various sections allowing the soloists to shine either on their own or in combination with the others. The work concludes with an elaborate setting of the "Glory be."

Laudate pueri

The *Laudate pueri* (Psalm 112) was written specifically for the feast of Our Lady of Mount Carmel in July 1707. It could have served either as the first psalm of first Vespers or the second psalm of second Vespers. Handel scores the music for soprano solo, choir, and orchestra. A solo oboe also plays a prominent role. The opening section is extremely rousing, with the stirring soprano opening being echoed by full choir. Handel may well have worked under pressure (he only finished this setting eight days before the feast!), but the result is one of his finest works. Once again, one can marvel at the assurance with which the young German Protestant sets Latin texts for an Italian audience.

Nisi Dominus

The *Nisi Dominus* (Psalm 126) was most likely sung as the fourth psalm at second Vespers for the feast of Our Lady of Mount Carmel. This setting was completed just three days before the feastday itself!

The opening is exquisite, with choir, orchestra, and soloists singing with quiet assurance "if the Lord does not build the house, in vain do the builders labour." The opening melody is unashamedly Gregorian in character. Once again, we are impressed by the ability of Handel to adapt his music to a different religious and cultural context. Many elements which became hallmarks of Handel's more mature years are already in evidence. We have an example of a "battle" aria with his setting of the words *Sicut sagittae*. The section *Cum dederit dilectis suis somnum* is another piece of "night" music. The concluding *Gloria patri* is as grand as the final section of Handel's later *Messiah*. Once again, the principal melody has a plainchant feel to it.

Handel also composed brief settings of the antiphons *Haec est regina* and *Te decus virginum*. These were most probably intended for first Vespers of the feast of Our Lady of Mount Carmel.

Conclusion

Handel's music for the Carmelites has been one of the most important re-discoveries in musical scholarship. But Handel's music is much more than an historical curiosity. If readers take time to listen to the music with imagination they will indeed find themselves transported back to an earlier era of Carmelite experience, but at the same time they will find much to sustain them in living the Carmelite vocation in the world of today. Words have a compelling force. But when words and music come together effectively the human spirit can be moved at an even deeper level to experience something of heaven on earth.

5

Felix Mendelssohn's *Elijah*

Oh rest in the Lord, wait patiently for him and He shall give thee thy heart's desires. Commit thy way unto Him, and trust in Him, and fret not thyself because of evil-doers.

These words, set to gentle music and sung by an angel, represent the still centre at the heart of Mendelssohn's highly dramatic *oratorio Elijah*. They are timely words of comfort to the dejected prophet of Carmel whose life has reached its lowest ebb: "O Lord, I have laboured in vain! Yea, I have spent my strength for naught! Oh, that I now might die!"

Taken as a whole, *Elijah* can be seen as a journey from darkness to light. The *oratorio* begins mysteriously with Elijah (a bass) singing this prologue: "As God the Lord of Israel liveth, before whom I stand: There shall not be dew nor rain these years, but according to my word." Mendelssohn uses a very dark orchestration to accompany the words of the prophet. He omits the stringed instruments of the orchestra and creates a dark and uneasy atmosphere using only wind and brass instruments with a shivery effect on the timpani (kettle drums). Even the melody Elijah sings has a creepy feel to it; Mendelssohn deliberately, makes the distances between the notes create a sense of doom (in music theory these spaces or "intervals" are known as diminished fifths). In contrast, when we come to the final chorus of the *oratorio* a total transformation has taken place. The key note used at the beginning of the prologue ("D" is the first note Elijah sings) is now part of a chorus of triumph which culminates in a jubilant "Amen" (the "D" is now part of a blazing chord of "D major").

So the whole of Mendelssohn's *Elijah* can be seen to move from initial darkness to its culmination in light. Such a movement from darkness to light reflects a transformation in Elijah (as the hero of the drama) and in the people of Israel. And one thing is sure, in setting the Elijah story from the First Book of Kings, Mendelssohn intended listeners in every age to be similarly transformed.

In recent years, the Carmelite Order has sought to deepen its understanding of its Elijan heritage. In doing so, Carmelites have gone back to the sources associated with the early years of the Order's existence (e.g. the *Rule of Carmel*, the "*Rubrica Prima*" to the First Constitutions and the *Book of the First Monks*). Again and again, Elijah emerges (along with Mary our mother and sister) as a vital inspiration for Carmelites who, as sons and daughters of Elijah, can readily appreciate the power of Mendelssohn's music.

Life of Mendelssohn[1]

Jakob Ludwig Felix Mendelssohn was born in the German city of Hamburg on 3 February 1809. His parents, Abraham and Leah, had already one daughter, Fanny, and were to have two further children, Rebecka and Paul. The family moved to Berlin in 1811 on account of the French occupation of Hamburg. At this time Abraham and Leah were Jews. However, Leah's brother had recently become a Christian and had taken the name of Bartholdy. Abraham and Leah decided to have their children baptised in 1816 (they themselves waited until 1822). From henceforth they would adopt the surname Mendelssohn Bartholdy.

The young Felix grew up in an extremely privileged and profoundly cultured environment. His grandfather was the great Jewish philosopher, Moses Mendelssohn. Both Felix and his sister Fanny were very gifted musically and came to be taught by some of the best music teachers of the time. Felix began composition lessons at the age of eight with Carl Zelter. In time it looked like he might pursue a career in music. Although his son's exceptional musical abilities received encouragement from family and friends, Abraham had some doubts about the desirability of Felix making music his profession. The boy was taken to see Luigi Cherubini at the Paris Conservatoire who attested to his giftedness and assured the father that his son would indeed have a promising career as a musician.

As a young man, Mendelssohn travelled widely. He went as far south as Naples and as far north as the Hebrides. Indeed Italy and Scotland were to provide the inspiration for two of his symphonies. He was city director of music in Dusseldorf and in 1835 became director of the prestigious Gewandhaus Orchestra in Leipzig. In Leipzig (the town associated with J. S. Bach) Mendelssohn flourished. He was unhappy after returning to Berlin at the invitation of King Friedrich Wilhelm IV in

---

1. For the life and works of Felix Mendelssohn, see Peter Mercer-Taylor, *The Life of Mendelssohn* (Cambridge: Cambridge University Press (Musical Lives Series), 2000) and R. Larry Todd, *Mendelssohn: A Life in Music* (Oxford: Oxford University Press, 2003); also Philip Radcliffe, *Mendelssohn*, revised edition (Oxford: Oxford University Press (Master Musicians Series), 2000).

Jakob Ludwig Felix Mendelssohn was born in Hamburg, Germany in February 1809. The young Felix grew up in an extremely privileged and profoundly cultured environment. As a young man, Mendelssohn travelled widely. At the age of thirty-eight, on November 4, 1847, he died.

1841. Returning once again to Leipzig in 1843, Mendelssohn established a music conservatory and spent his final years there until his death at the age of thirty-eight on 4 November 1847, six months after the death of his beloved sister, Fanny.

Mendelssohn and his *Elijah*[2]

As early as 1837 Mendelssohn had begun to plan an *oratorio* on the subject of the prophet Elijah. His first *oratorio*, *Saint Paul*, had been a tremendous success some months previously. For the next few years he regularly discussed his ideas with two literary friends, Carl Klingerman and Julius Schubring. In June 1845 Mendelssohn received a commission for a new *oratorio* from the Birmingham Festival Committee in England. Schubring worked as his librettist in preparing a German text, and the music was completed in 1846. Mendelssohn and his librettist changed the order of some of the episodes in the Elijah story for the sake of dramatic effect. They also inserted material. On the whole, however, Mendelssohn and Schubring were very faithful to the text of Scripture.

Mendelssohn corresponded regularly with one William Bartholomew in the preparation of an English translation of the libretto for Elijah. The first performance took place at Birmingham Town Hall on 26 August 1846 with Mendelssohn himself conducting. *Elijah* was a complete success and was received enthusiastically by critics and public alike. For his part, Mendelssohn was dissatisfied with some parts of the *oratorio*. For instance, he rewrote the scene with the widow. His final version received several performances in England. The second performance on 23 April 1847 was even attended by Queen Victoria and Prince Albert.

Some listeners express surprise that the gentle arid refined Felix Mendelssohn Bartholdy chose the character of Elijah, prophet of Carmel and the fiercest and most vengeful of all the Old Testament prophets. Mendelssohn was a convinced Lutheran Christian, but it has to be recognised that Jewishness would always remain an important part of his identity (just as Jewishness remained an important part of the identity of the later Carmelite, Edith Stein). Commentators and listeners alike have long identified a strong Jewish "lilt" in Mendelssohn's music (take the famous violin concerto for example). Some scholars have made a convincing case for the Jewish origins of certain melodies employed by Mendelssohn in *Elijah,* e.g., "Lord, bow Thine ear".

However, apart from a general identification with Judaism there is a more profound aspect to Mendelssohn's choice of Elijah as a subject for his *oratorio*. Mendelssohn was a very principled man who was convinced that his time was in need of reform. He was utterly disenchanted with the corruption and court intrigue at Berlin which had interfered with his

---

2.   See the excellent notes by Nicholas Temperley which accompany the CD-version of the recording of Mendelssohn's *Elijah* conducted by Paul Daniel (see list of recordings at the end of this volume for details).

plans for a musical revival. In a letter to Schubring he says: "I imagined Elijah as a real prophet through and through, of the kind we could really do with today: strong, zealous and yes, even bad-tempered, angry and brooding– in contrast to the riff-raff, whether of the court or of the people, and indeed at odds with almost the whole world –and yet borne aloft as if on angel's wings."[3]

Mendelssohn and His Audience

There can be little doubt that Mendelssohn intended his *Elijah* for a British audience. Although the music was originally written for a German text he took constant care to consult his translator concerning the nuances of the English language. He even adjusted the music to make sure it fitted the English words.

It has to be recognised that his original English audience saw "*the Elijah*" (as they called it) as something of an anti-Roman Catholic work. John Henry Newman had only recently converted to Roman Catholicism (in 1845) and feeling was running high among Nonconformists and Evangelical Anglicans alike. Some were suspicious of the Oxford Movement with its espousal of Anglo-Catholicism. Alied to this, many Victorian listeners were worried about the apparent erosion of faith that had come with the growth of rationalism and scientific progress. Nicholas Temperley reflects:

> So when the devout Victorian witnessed the destruction of Baal and the discomforture of Ahab and Jezebel, he could take satisfaction in the punishment of all who threatened his beliefs, whether they were Roman "idolaters" or heathen "scoffers." The reassertion of stern Old Testament morality was in perfect harmony with the dissenting tradition, going back to the early Puritans. Victorian audiences, as more than one observer noted, were apt to treat an *oratorio* concert almost as an act of worship.[4]

Mendelssohn cannot have been unaware of his audience's preoccupations. However, it is unlikely he shared their evangelical piety in any kind of simplistic manner. He generally preferred to see his Elijah as an example of the kind of leadership needed for a thorough moral reform of his day. There is certainly no evidence to suggest that Mendelssohn himself saw his work as anti-Catholic. It is one of the great strengths of *Elijah*

---

3.   Quoted in Nicholas Temperley, *op. cit.*, p. 12.
4.   *Ibid.*, p. 13.

that it can appeal to audiences in any age. Elijah, prophet of Carmel, will always challenge audiences wherever and whenever Mendelssohn's *oratorio* is performed. He will always be the bane of complacency and smugness. He will always both confound and inspire.

ELIJAH – PART I

Drought[5]

The ominous Prologue (marked *grave* in the score) to Mendelssohn's *Elijah* corresponds exactly to the first appearance of Elijah in 1 Kings 17: Elijah foretells the drought that is to come. This dark prelude is followed by an energetic overture for full orchestra which leads into the first chorus without a break.

The first chorus for full choir is extremely loud (marked *fortissimo* in the score). The people shout: "Help, Lord! Wilt Thou quite destroy us?" The full brunt of the drought is being felt: "The deeps afford no water! And the rivers are exhausted." At one point the vigorous music abates to allow two sopranos to sing in dialogue with the choir: "Zion spreadeth her hands for aid, and there is neither help nor comfort."

There follows a brief quasi-spoken interjection (recitative) by Obadiah, exhorting the people to abandon the worship of idols. Obadiah, a servant of Elijah, proceeds to sing the first of the famous solo arias of Mendelssohn's *oratorio*:

"If with all your hearts ye truly seek Me, ye shall ever surely find Me." However, the people are still full of woe and sing in chorus: "Yet doth the Lord see it not." At the words "his curse hath fallen upon us" we hear once again the dread music of the prologue. Some commentators call this dark melody the "curse motif."

Elijah at the wadi Carith[6]

An angel (contralto) commands Elijah: "Elijah! Get thee hence, Elijah! Depart and turn eastward: thither hide thee by Cherith's brook. There shalt thou drink its waters; and the Lord thy God hath commanded the ravens to feed thee there: so do according unto His word." This is followed by a touching double quartet for two sopranos, two altos, two tenors, and two basses: "For he shall give His angels charge over thee."

---

5.   1 Kings 17: 1.
6.   1 Kings 17: 1-6.

Closeup of the carved wooden statue of the Prophet Elijah on the main altar of the main chapel at the Monastery of Mount Carmel in Niagara Falls, Ontario. Mendelssohn is thought to have seen Elijah as an example of the kind of leadership needed for a thorough moral reform of his day.

Elijah and the Widow[7]

The angel then orders Elijah to go Zarephath. There he shall meet a widow who will feed him. The scene is set for what musically proves to be a moving dialogue and duet between the widow (soprano) and Elijah. Indeed more than one commentator has pointed to the operatic qualities of this episode. At first, the widow is too distraught to be able to welcome Elijah with any enthusiasm. Her son is dead. However, Elijah implores the Lord to bring the son back to life: "God, let the spirit of this child return, that he again may live!" He tries several times in vain and each time the widow replies scornfully. Finally, we know something is about to happen. On the third attempt, we hear a trumpet fanfare accompanying Elijah's cry. The son is revived and the widow sings: "The Lord hath heard thy prayer, the soul of my son reviveth; my son reviveth!" There follows a quasi-passionate duet (although this is not a love duet!) between Elijah and the widow. She has recognised Elijah as a man of God and her recognition leads them to praise God together. This is followed by the choir singing of the graciousness and compassion of God. For the first time the choir sings gently. The music bubbles and runs along registering in the music that a transformation has taken place through the intercession of Elijah.

Elijah and the Prophets of Baal[8]

The next episode concerns Elijah's challenge to Ahab and to the prophets of Baal and their followers: "Then we shall see whose God is the Lord." In the music there is a huge climax at the word "whose God is the Lord." It is as if there is no doubt as to the identity of the true God. Several times the prophets call on Baal to send down fire and each time to no avail. Finally, gently and mysteriously Elijah sings: "Draw near, all ye people, come to me." He begins to sing a warm and tender aria (in contrast to all the huffing and puffing of the Baal worshippers): "Lord God of Abraham, Isaac and Israel, let it be known that Thou art God, and that I am Thy servant!" This is followed by a quartet of angels singing "cast thy burden upon the Lord, and He shall sustain thee." Elijah then calls on his Lord to send down fire. A terrifying chorus ensues: "The fire descends from heaven! The flames consume his offering." The prophets of Baal are routed and consumed by fire.

---

7.   1 Kings 17: 7-16.
8.   1 Kings 18: 20-39.

The Little Cloud[9]

Obadiah pleads with Elijah to ask for rain. The prophet of Carmel sings: "Open the heavens and send us relief. Help, help Thy servant now, O God!" The people echo his words in chorus: "Open the heavens and send us relief." Then three times (fewer times than in the scriptural account) Elijah sends a boy (a boy soprano in the score) to see if there is any sign of rain. Brass fanfares accompany Elijah's final plea signalling that something is beginning to happen. The boy sings: "Behold, a little cloud ariseth now from the waters; it is like a man's hand! The heavens are black with cloud and with wind; the storm rusheth louder and louder!" The people respond with delight and Elijah sings: "Thanks be to God! For He is gracious; and His mercy endureth for evermore!" Part one of the *oratorio* ends with the exultant chorus: "Thanks be to God!"

ELIJAH – PART II

Part II of the *oratorio* begins (in manner reminiscent of Bach's *Saint Matthew Passion* with the famous soprano aria "Hear ye, Israel." We know that Mendelssohn intended this aria for one particular soprano. The first note (F sharp) was apparently her best. This aria is followed by another rousing chorus: "Be not afraid."

Queen Jezebel[10]

In the next scene Elijah has another go at Ahab and incurs the wrath of Queen Jezebel (whose part is sung by a contralto). This particular scene is rather operatic in style (reminding us of the earlier scene with the widow). Jezebel condemns Elijah to death. The people echo her condemnation with relish: "He shall perish," they sing.

Elijah in the Wilderness[11]

Elijah has had enough. To music laden with doom he sings (in reply to Obadiah): "I journey hence to the wilderness." There follows possibly the most moving aria of the whole *oratorio* "It is enough!" The words and music fit together in a most heart-wrenching manner. They whole effect is strengthened by aching phrases on the cello which weave their way into the rest of the music. Eventually, Elijah falls asleep and a tenor sings: "See, now he sleepeth beneath a juniper tree in the wilderness, but

9.   1 Kings 18: 41-46.
10.   1 Kings 19: 1-2.
11.   1 Kings 19: 3-6.

the angels of the Lord encamp round about all them that fear him." At this point, three angels sing the famous trio "Lift thine eyes to the mountains, whence cometh help." Commentators often single out this chorus for its beauty and poetry and for its lack of sentimentality. An angel appears to Elijah and commands him to journey to Horeb, the mountain of the Lord: "Forty days and forty nights shalt thou go."

Mount Horeb[12]

Elijah does not seem to be very comforted by the words of the angel. In fact, his response is angry: "O Lord, I have laboured in vain! Yea, I have spent my strength for naught!" He even sings: "Oh, that I now might die!" It is at this point that the angel sings the well-known aria "Oh rest in the Lord." It is in total contrast to the angry and hopeless words of Elijah. The words of the angel are full of tenderness and reassuring strength. It is small wonder that this aria has often been sung at funerals. The chorus echoes the words of the angel: "He that shall endure to the end, shall be saved."

Night is falling and Elijah sings: "Night falleth round me, O Lord! Be Thou not far from me! Hide not Thy face, O Lord, from me, my soul is thirsting for Thee, as a thirsty land." It is interesting to note that at this point the music echoes the music of the opening chorus of the *oratorio* (where the people sing of drought). The angel urges him to go to stand on the mountain before the Lord: "Thy face must be veiled, for He draweth near." In one of the most memorable moments of the *oratorio* the chorus sing of the theophany on Horeb. The Lord is not in the tempest, He is not in the earthquake, and He is not in the fire. Finally the chorus sing: "And after the fire there came a still small voice. And in that still voice onward came the Lord." This music depicting the wind, the earthquake, and the fire has tremendous vigour, urgency, and attack. Yet Mendelssohn is able to achieve a gentle serenity in the music which accompanies the "still small voice" of the Lord.

Conclusion

After the manifestation of the Lord on Horeb, there is a series of choruses and arias emphasising the transformation that has taken place in the prophet of Carmel. He is now strengthened for his ongoing mission: "I go on my way in the strength of the Lord. For Thou art my Lord, and I will suffer for Thy sake. My heart is therefore glad, my glory rejoiceth;

---

12.   1 Kings 19: 7-13.

and my flesh shall also rest in hope." The chorus describing Elijah's ascent into heaven is particularly effective. Mendelssohn uses some daring changes of key at the passage describing the chariot of fire and the horse. The penultimate number in the *oratorio* is a quartet: "Oh come everyone that thirsteth, oh come to the waters, oh come unto Him! Oh hear, and your souls shall live for ever." Just before Mendelssohn launches into the closing triumphant chorus, he quotes once again the dreaded music of the prologue (the "curse motif"). The effect is to remind us that the lives of the people of Israel have been transformed by the saving work of their Lord and God. The people have been brought from darkness into light. And such transformation has also worked on a personal level in the life of the prophet Elijah who has learned much about discerning the presence of the Lord amidst the apparent darkness of his time. The final chorus is a blaze of light: "And then shall your light break forth as the light of morning breaketh: and your health shall speedily spring forth then: and the glory of the Lord shall reward you. Lord, Our Creator, how excellent Thy Name is in all the nations! Thou fillest heaven with Thy glory. Amen." It is clearly Mendelssohn's intention that these final movements look forward to the coming of Christ.

Elijah: A Man for All Seasons

In common with generations of Carmelites, Felix Mendelssohn saw Elijah as a profound challenge to contemporary moral decay and social-political corruption. Mendelssohn was also sensitive to the contemplative dimension of Elijah's life (just listen to the more reflective arias and gentle recitatives). For Mendelssohn, Elijah is a man for all seasons, whose fiery words and deeds can have a profound impact, transcending the limitations of time and place. It remains for the reader to listen and to discover the compelling power of Mendelssohn's *Elijah* at first hand.

◊ ◊ ◊

6

Venerable Augustine Mary of the Blessed Sacrament (Hermann Cohen), OCD

Early Life[1]

Hermann Cohen was born on 10 November 1821 at 189 Ellern-torbrucke, Neustadt, Hamburg, in Northern Germany. He was the second of four surviving children born to Abraham Cohen and Rosalie Benjamin; two other children died young. The Cohens, prosperous Jewish bankers with links to the Rothschilds, were one of the richest families in Hamburg at the time.

Young Cohen began to learn the piano at the age of four. He showed early and immense promise, soon outstripping his older brother, Albert, who was also learning the instrument. Cohen could early on play tunes from the operas and extemporise with skill. He gave his first public concerts at Altona and Frankfurt at the age of seven.

Cohen's parents belonged to the Reformed branch of Judaism.[2] In later years, after his conversion to Christianity, Cohen was fond of recalling that "Cohen" meant "priest." There is some early indication of a certain religious sensibility on his part. In his *Confessions*, Cohen recalled his early attraction to worship at the Synagogue: "When I saw the Rabbi mount the steps of the sanctuary, draw the curtain and open the door, I waited expectantly."[3]

---

1. For the life and work of Hermann Cohen, OCD, see Timothy (Tadgh) Tierney, OCD, *The Story of Hermann Cohen* (Boar's Hill, Oxford: The Teresian Press, 1996) and *A Life of Hermann Cohen: from Franz Liszt to John of the Cross* (Bloomington, IN: Balboa Press, 2017). The account of Herman Cohen in the current chapter is heavily indebted to these two works.

2. Reformed Judaism (sometimes called 'Liberal' or 'Progressive' Judaism) is a major denomination within Judaism that emphasises the evolving nature of faith, the primacy of the ethical over the ceremonial and the ongoing nature of revelation which is not exclusively focused on the theophany on Mount Sinai.

3. Quoted Tierney, *The Story*, p. 10. The quotation is taken from a document called the *Confessions* (recalling Saint Augustine) which was written by Herman Cohen at the request of his superiors during his novitiate year. It is frequently quoted in the first biography of Cohen by Canon Charles Sylvain but, unfortunately, is now lost. Sylvain's biography was translated into English with the title *The Life of Father Hermann* (New York: P.J. Kennedy and Sons, 1925). The French original was published in 2009 with the title *Flamme Ardente au Carmel* (Flavigny: Traditions Monastiques, 2009).

At the age of twelve, Cohen's mother decided to take him to Paris so he could get the best possible musical training at the famous Conservatory. As the family were experiencing severe financial difficulties at the time, Rosalie sought the patronage of the Grand Dukes George of Mecklenburg-Strelitz and Francis I of Mecklenburg-Schwerin; these were neighbouring duchies in the north of Germany near to Hamburg. Successful in her attempts to gain sponsorship, she moved with her four children to Paris in July 1834.

Franz Liszt[4]

Unfortunately, as Cohen was not French-born, he was denied admission to the Paris Conservatory. Not to be put off, Rosalie approached the renowned pianist, Franz Liszt (1811-1886), asking him to take her son as a pupil. At first, Liszt was reluctant but was persuaded enough on hearing the young Cohen play. Cohen soon became a member of Liszt's close circle which included such "colourful" characters as the author George Sand (1804-1876) and the renegade priest, the Abbé de Lammenais (1782-1854). Liszt's own teacher, Carl Czerny (1791-1857), had nicknamed him *Putzig* (meaning "funny" or "cute"). Cohen quickly came to be known by the diminutive *Puzzi* ("cute little guy") among the members of Liszt's circle: George Sand liked to call him *le mélancolique Puzzi* (the melancholic Puzzi). He gave his first important concert in Paris in April 1835.

In June 1834 Liszt eloped to Geneva with his new lover, the Countess Marie d'Agoult and began to teach at the fledgling music Conservatory there. Cohen persuaded Liszt to allow him to move to Switzerland with him. Liszt continued to teach him and entrusted ten of his own students to his star pupil who at fifteen years of age became an official piano professor at the Conservatory.

Cohen travelled with Liszt on many trips through the Swiss countryside. Around this time Cohen attested to having had a profound religious experience on hearing Liszt play the organ at the cathedral in Fribourg, where he improvised on the *Dies irae* theme from Mozart's *Requiem*.

In 1837 Liszt and his circle returned to Paris. Young Cohen was now sixteen years of age and all was not well. He had developed extravagant tastes, and the combination of a lavish lifestyle and a liking for gambling meant he had incurred very significant debts. Cohen gives us a powerful insight into his initial attraction to gambling and the subsequent impact

4.   For the life and work of Franz Liszt, see Derek Watson, *Liszt* (Oxford: Oxford University Press [Master Musicians Series], 2001).

Hermann Cohen was born in November 1821 in Hamburg. Cohen soon became a member of Franz Liszt's close circle of students, following Liszt to Geneva. At age 15 he became a piano professor at the Geneva Conservatory. Following his conversion to Catholicism in 1847 he entered the Discalced Carmelite Order. He became a famous preacher in France and in various cities of Europe. He is credited with assisting in the restoration of the Order in France. Besides fame as an exceptional musician, Cohen's ministry was also renown.

it had on his life:

> I think it was the first time I had ever seen this sort of game, and I eagerly followed the fortunes of the players. Large sums of money were lost and won. I asked if I might try something myself. It was there that the vice which ruled the best years of my life originated. It didn't give me a moment's rest and often drove me to the verge of suicide because of the enormous losses I sustained.[5]

The fact that he had developed a romantic attachment to a married woman led to the attempts on the part of the Countess d'Agout to discredit Cohen in Liszt's eyes; previously Cohen had become engaged to a French pianist which came to nothing. The efforts of the Countess notwithstanding, Cohen continued to accompany Liszt on his concert

5. Quoted Tierney, *The Story*, p. 20.

tours around Europe until 1840. However, following a concert tour to Dresden in 1841, Cohen fell out with Liszt when the young man was accused of embezzling funds from his master. Cohen could not persuade Liszt of his innocence. For the next five years, he travelled around Europe with his mother and his sister, Henriette, composing piano pieces and giving concerts.

Return to Paris and Conversion

Cohen moved to Paris in 1846 where he began a relationship with the circus performer, dancer, theatre director, and writer, Céleste Mogador (1824-1909). However, Cohen ended the affair abruptly. He had begun to have a series of religious experiences and felt drawn to God. He was disgusted with his life and sought spiritual advice and spent long hours praying in the churches of the French capital. Céleste's diary is interesting. First, it gives an insight into Cohen as a performing artist:

> There was a request for music and a young man sat down at the piano. As soon as he began to play I recognised an expert. He was fair with blue eyes, slightly protruding lips and white teeth. His hands worked the keyboard with incredible lightness and agility. It was not like music but really a melody that went straight to the heart." [6]

Secondly, Céleste's diary (although a little inaccurate on points of detail), witnesses to the change that was taking place in Cohen's life:

> One day I saw him enter the church of the Madeleine where he stayed for two hours. He seemed depressed and soon after I had a letter from him in which he said that his life was no longer his own and that his trust in God was growing, in whom he was finding support. But when I asked to see him again he declined. Later I heard the unusual news that after we parted he left for Italy, visited Rome, became a Catholic and entered a monastery. I was very disappointed myself although I did not admit it. [7]

Rather like Saint Augustine before him, Cohen's conversion was something of a slow process:

> Yes. I already knew Jesus Christ, I saw him, I felt him, felt his touch on every page I read, in every hymn I sang and in every Catholic service I attended. I understood I must break the chains that bound me and walk towards him but I was unable to do so. I made resolutions in the morning which were gone in the evening. I resisted temptation in the evening only to give in by morning. [8]

6.   *Ibid.*, p. 29-30.
7.   *Ibid.*, p. 30.
8.   *Ibid.*, p. 30.

In May 1847, while playing the organ for Benediction at the church of Saint Valère (he was deputising for the regular music director), Cohen experienced a strong call to become a Christian: "*I felt something deep within me as if I had found myself. It was like the prodigal son facing himself.I was automatically bowing my head.When I returned the following Friday the same thing happened and I thought of becoming a Catholic.*" [9]

This continued for some time, becoming stronger when he was on a concert tour to Ems, Germany: Cohen felt overwhelmed on attending church services in a local church there and wrote of the "inner joy" he felt at the time.

Cohen was introduced to a convert from Judaism and priest, Marie-Théodore Ratisbonne (1802-1834) who in his turn brought him into contact with the Abbé Legrande. Having received instruction from Legrande, Cohen was baptised on 28 August 1847, the Feast of Saint Augustine, taking Marie-Augustin-Henri as his baptismal name.

Cohen attests to his having had an overwhelming experience of divine love at his baptism accompanied by a vision of Christ, the Blessed Virgin Mary and a multitude of saints, all bathed in heavenly light. He gives this account of his mystical experience:

> A gentle warmth penetrated me and, in spite of the brilliant light which radiated from all sides, my gaze never tired of plunging into the rays of light … for deep within there was an even brighter light … and there stood a glorious throne and seated on the throne was Our Lord Jesus Christ, beautiful with eternal youth, with his beloved mother on his right and around his feet a host of saints clothed in the brightest colours of the rainbow." [10]

Cohen received the Sacrament of Confirmation on 3 December from the Archbishop of Paris (and Servant of God), Denis Auguste Affre (1793-1848). It is interesting to note how Cohen was also developing a sense of the importance of the active apostolate around the time of his conversion: he became involved with helping the poor through Blessed Frederick Ozanam (1813-1853), the founder of the Saint Vincent de Paul Society.

Cohen felt he had a vocation to the priesthood. He first approached the Benedictine monks at the Abbey of Solesmes, famous for their re-vival of plainchant; they declined his application. He next turned to the Dominican Jean-Baptiste Henri Lacordaire (1802-1861) who was re-establishing his Order in France. Lacordaire recommended that Cohen

---

9.   *Ibid.*, p. 31.
10.   *Ibid.*, p. 34.

find a more monastic order than the Dominicans. It was at this time that Cohen came to know the Discalced Carmelite friars and felt attracted to join them. The fact that he was a recent convert meant that a special dispensation was sought and eventually obtained from Rome.

Discalced Carmelite Friar

Cohen gave a farewell concert in order to clear his debts before joining the Order. He entered the Discalced Carmelite novitiate at Le Broussey in Rions on 16 July, the Feast of Our Lady of Mount Carmel, in 1848. He received the religious habit on 6 October 1849 and was given the religious name Augustine Mary of the Blessed Sacrament. He made his profession on 7 October 1850 and began the course of studies for ordination. Cohen struggled somewhat with his studies: his formal education had ended when he was ten years of age. He required certain exemptions and was finally ordained to the priesthood on 19 April 1851. Cohen came to be in rumental in the restoration of the Discalced Carmelites in France. He had an important role in the founding of priories at Bagnères-de-Bigorre (1853), Lyon (1857), and a hermitage in Tarasteix, near Lourdes (1857). It is interesting to note how Cohen, as a musician, ensured that the church of the priory at Bagnères-de-Bigorre was provided with an organ by the most prestigious French organ builder of the day, Aristide Cavaillé-Coll.[11] Later on, the church of the priory he founded at Kensington in London would have an instrument by the same firm.

Bernadette of Lourdes

Cohen, as we have just noted, established a hermitage at Tarasteix, near Lourdes in 1857. The following year Our Lady appeared several times to Saint Bernadette Soubirous (1844-1879). The final apparition took place on the Feast of Our Lady of Mount Carmel, 16 July 1858. Cohen visited Lourdes in September of the same year and by dint of persistent petitioning of local authorities was permitted to visit the grotto. On this visit to Lourdes he had the privileged opportunity of meeting young Bernadette and evidently had a lengthy conversation with her. Cohen lent the young girl a sympathetic ear, it would seem, at a time when many doubted the veracity of her claims to have seen Our Lady.[12]

11.   The organ is now located in the Church of Saint Martin, Castelnau d'Estrètefonds in the Haute Garonne department in southwestern France .

12.   For the affinities between Saint Bernadette Soubirous and the Carmelites, see Tierney, *The Story*, pp. 70-71 and Tierney, *A Life*, pp. 144-145. It would seem that Saint Bernadette in later years recalled Hermann Cohen with approval.

Famed Preacher

After his ordination, Cohen became a famous preacher in France and in several cities of Europe.[13] He preached to thousands of people at Geneva, Bordeaux, Lyon (where he drew a crowd of three thousand people), Tours, Béziers, Montpellier, and Avignon. Cohen preached at the church of Saint Louis of France in Rome. In Paris, he drew huge crowds at the churches of Saint-Sulpice and Sainte-Clotilde. The travelling required by the preaching apostolate led Cohen to refer to himself jokingly as "the wandering Jew."[14] Once when someone asked him where he lived, he replied: "In a railway carriage!"[15] Later, at the times of his English sojourn, Cohen preached in Scotland and Ireland. He wrote from Waterford in the south of Ireland:

> I received your letter in the south of Ireland in Waterford, where I found to my great joy, a people fired by a great Catholic spirit, so alive that I could have believed I was living among the early Christians. Yesterday I had nine thousand listeners. I have never seen such great faith."[16]

On a visit to Dublin, Cohen preached at the Church of Saint Teresa in Clarendon Street.

Devotion to the Eucharist

Nocturnal Adoration

One aspect of Cohen's life and spirituality requiring special attention is his devotion to the Eucharist. In the year after his conversion and baptism, he was visiting the chapel of the Carmelite Sisters in Paris where the Blessed Sacrament was exposed. There was a group of women present. When one of the sisters politely asked Cohen to leave, as she was about to lock the chapel, he gently enquired why the women were remaining. The sister explained that they would pray all night. This made a major impression on Cohen who, together with a number of his friends, shortly afterwards set up the Association of Nocturnal Adorers at the church of Our Lady of Victories in Paris. To this day a plaque at the church commemorates Cohen's initiative. Furthermore, the current altar

---

13. For the texts of a number of Cohen's sermons (including at the Paris churches of Saint-Sulpice and Sainte-Clotilde) and other writings see Tierney, *A Life*, pp. 209-338.

14. Quoted Tierney, *The Story*, p. 55.

15. *Ibid.* This might put one in mind of Blessed Titus Brandsma, O. Carm. about whom it was said: "He was the mystic on the Continent of Europe who had a season's railroad ticket and who became holy in train compartments." (Quoted by Jacobus Melsen, O. Carm., "Mysticism: The Aim of the Life of Titus Brandsma (1881-1942)" in Redemptus Maria Valabek, O. Carm., *Essays on Titus Brandsma: Carmelite, Educator, Journalist, Martyr* (Rome: Edizioni Carmelitane, 1985), p. 100-114, p. 100)

16. Quoted in Tierney, *The Story*, p. 78-79.

of the now Basilica of Our Lady of Victories contains panels commemo-
rating both Venerable Hermann Cohen and Saint Thérèse of Lisieux.
Saint Thérèse was cured on 13 May 1883, during the course of a novena
of Masses being offered there.[17] She tells in her autobiography how Our
Lady smiled at her and cured her. Later, in 1887, she returned to the
church with her father on her way to Rome to pray in thanksgiving. It
was due to the association with Saint Thérèse that Pope Pius XI raised
the church to the status of basilica in 1927. Around the time of his en-
try to Carmel, Cohen developed a friendship with Saint Julien Eymard
(1811-1868), founder of the Blessed Sacrament Fathers. The Curé of
Ars, Saint John Vianney (1786-1859), was one who greatly encouraged
Cohen in his endeavours to promote devotion to the Eucharist.

Importance of the Prayer After Reception of Communion

It is important to note that, in addition to placing a major emphasis
on devotion to the Eucharist through adoration, Cohen also strongly
advocated the regular reception of Communion and, furthermore, the
importance of prayer after Communion; indeed he spoke concerning
the regular reception of Holy Communion in his first sermon after
ordination. In Chapter 6 of Saint John's Gospel Jesus says: "Whoever
eats my flesh and drinks my blood lives in me and I live in them. As
the living Father serves me and I draw life from the Father, so whoever
eats me will draw life from me." Following this, Saint Teresa of Avila
strongly advocated prayer after Communion, on receiving the Eucharist
within oneself, as an opportunity for the gift of contemplation.[18] It is
also a major part of the spirituality of Blessed Titus Brandsma.[19] This is

17.   Saint Thérèse of Lisieux, [MS A, III] *Story of A Soul: The Autobiography of Saint Thérèse of Lisieux*, transl. John Clarke, OCD, 3rd edition (Washington DC: ICS Publications, 1996), p. 65ff.

18.   For Teresa of Avila, receiving Christ in Holy Communion was an experience of communion with Christ, a union with Christ. And, above all, for Teresa the time after communion was a time of intimacy, a time to be with the Lord, her beloved. She writes: "One day after receiving Communion, it seemed most clear to me that our Lord sat beside me; and He began to console me with great favors and He told me among other things, 'See Me here, daughter, for it is I; give Me your hands.' And it seemed he took them and placed them on His side and said, 'Behold my wounds. You are not without Me. This short life is passing away.'" (Teresa of Avila, *Spiritual Testimonies*, 12, 6 in Kieran Kavanaugh, OCD and Otilio Rodriguez, OCD, transl., *The Collected Works of Saint Teresa of Avila*, vol. I, 2nd edition (Washington, DC: ICS Publications, 1987, p. 390). On another occasion, Teresa warns her sisters of not underestimating the power of the prayer after communion: "Now then, Sisters, consider that if in the beginning you do not fare well... the devil will make you think you find more devotion in other things and less in this recollection after Communion. Do not abandon this practice; the Lord will see in it how much you love Him." (Teresa of Avila, *The Way of Perfection*, Chapter 35, 2 in Kieran Kavanaugh, OCD and Otilio Rodriguez, OCD, transl., *The Collected Works of Saint Teresa of Avila*, vol. II, (Washington, DC: ICS Publications, 1980, p. 175). For Teresa, our prayer after Communion is for us an opportunity for recollection, for intimacy with the Lord. It is also a contemplative moment.

19.   Blessed Titus Brandsma, O. Carm., connects the prayer of thanksgiving of the communicant with Elijah, Prophet of Carmel: "In the school of Carmel the mystical contemplative life is the fruit of the Eucharistic life... The miraculous bread ministered to [Elijah] is a perfect image of that Eucharistic

because, in the Carmelite tradition, the interior and internal reception of the reality and mystery of the Eucharist is important. For his part, Cohen writes:"*Peace is a gift of the Holy Spirit which one obtains by fidelity to prayer and through prolonged thanksgiving after Holy Communion.*" [20] Elsewhere he says: "*Dedicate yourself a quarter of an hour to thanksgiving after Holy Communion and maintain yourself in peace, united to our dear Jesus, without trying to say a great number of prayers. One word suffices: Love.*" [21]

Influence on the Eucharistic Spirituality of Blessed Charles de Foucauld

Blessed Charles de Foucauld (1858-1916) was directly influenced by the writings of Venerable Hermann Cohen. There are certain affinities between the conversion stories of two men: Charles de Foucauld's own conversion began in the Paris church of Saint Augustin. De Foucauld knew and admired Cohen's hymns and often sang them. In his spiritual notes written in the Holy Land (1897-1900) he copied the following stanza from one of Cohen's motets on the Eucharist entitled "One thing I ask of the Lord":

As this flickering flame,

lit by faith unswerving,

which burns both day and night

before thy altar throne,

so may my hear, my God,

before thee self-consuming,

become at last all thine own,

become at last all thine own. [22]

Charles de Foucauld dedicated himself to the Sacred Heart at the

food, in the strength of which we walk in life's journey here below. The special cult of the Holy Sacrament has not been confined to Carmel, but we can say that it has always been a constant and important part of our Carmelite tradition. This in outline is the Eucharistic tradition of Carmel. With Elijah, we walk in the strength of that divine bread and since we want to come closer to the life of God in prayer, we must always remember Our Lord's command: 'Unless you eat the Flesh of the Son of Man and drink His Blood, you cannot have life in you.' Just as the communion of Elijah in the miraculous bread of the desert led him in his journey to the contemplation of God on Horeb, so too, the Holy Eucharist must lead us to the contemplation of His Holy Face. In the caves of Horeb God spoke gentle, whispering wind. The Lord was not in the storm nor in the earthquake, but in the gentle wind. So after Communion we must contemplate under the Eucharist we have received and in the depths of our heart; for now God passes." (Titus Brandsma, O. Carm., *The Beauty of Carmel* (Dublin: Clonmore and Reynolds, 1955), pp. 31-32).

20.   Tierney, *A Life*, Part II (Writings), p. 323.
21.   *Ibid.*
22.   Quoted Tierney, *The Story*, p. 40, n. 1.

Basilica of the Sacré-Coeur in Paris, a church where to this day the tradition of night adoration is observed.

Reconciliation with Franz Liszt

In 1851, at the time of Cohen's ordination, he and Liszt had begun to exchange letters, thereby renewing their association. Liszt even expressed a wish to be able to visit his former student in France. He was, however, unable to travel from Weimar in Germany where he lived. In June 1862 both Cohen and Liszt happened to be in Rome. Liszt was now a cleric himself, having taken minor orders and become a Franciscan tertiary. He and Cohen spent three weeks together in Rome, giving an impromptu piano recital together for the benefit of the Carmelite community and participating in the solemn Stations of the Cross at the Colosseum.

Mission to England

Also present in Rome in 1862 was the Archbishop of Westminster, Cardinal Nicholas Wiseman. Cohen's immense reputation as a preacher led to his being sent to England by Pope Pius IX, at the request of Wiseman, to re-establish a Carmelite presence there. The Carmelite had a private audience with the Pontiff who said to him: "I bless you my son, and I am sending you to England, as in the seventh century one of my predecessors blessed and sent the monk Augustine, the first apostle of that country."[23] Cohen arrived in London in 1862. He opened a new priory in Kensington, London on 16 October, the Feast of Saint Teresa of Avila, that year. Initially, the Carmelites were given the use of a small house which belonged to the Assumption Sisters at Kensington Square. Eventually, a more suitable property (a house with a garden) at the corner of Duke's Lane and Vicarage Place, Kensington (later Church Street) was rented and eventually purchased.

Cardinal Manning laid the foundation stone for a new church in the garden of the priory on 16 July 1865. The church, designed by Edward Welby Pugin (1834-1875) and dedicated to Our Lady of Mount Carmel and Saint Simon Stock (whose relics were brought personally from Bordeaux by Cohen), was completed in just one year and opened on 16 July, the Feast of Our Lady of Mount Carmel, 1866. Bishop Grant of Southwark sang the High Mass, Cardinal Manning presided and the Irish-born Jesuit, Peter Gallwey, preached the sermon. The new Cavaillé-Coll organ was inaugurated by the leading French organists Charles-

---

23.   *Ibid.*, p. 74.

Marie Widor and Alexandre Guilmant (1837-1911).[24] The choir sang Mozart's *Ave verum* and Arcadelt's *Ave Maria* for the occasion. That music was a priority for Cohen is clear from a letter to his sister at the time: "*Our celebrations to mark the inauguration were splendid, consoling and well attended. We have a beautiful church and an excellent organ by Cavaillé, and many debts! However, those are Saint Joseph's affair.*"[25]

Cohen came to public attention in England in 1864 when he and two other Carmelites gave spiritual assistance to five Catholic sailors who had been convicted of piracy and murder and who were about to be hanged at the Old Bailey. The report in the evening edition of *The Times* newspaper remarked on the scene of three Roman Catholic priests, tonsured and wearing stoles, mounting the scaffold to tend to the condemned men.

Return to France

In 1868 Cohen returned to France and retired to the hermitage at Tarasteix, near Lourdes, which he had earlier founded there. His eyesight began to fail and he was diagnosed with glaucoma. He made a pilgrimage to Lourdes. Bathing his eyes in the waters there for several days, Cohen's sight was miraculously restored. He returned to his hermitage having received a full cure.[26] Cohen's peace was disturbed by the outbreak of the Franco-Prussian War in 1870 which led to the expulsion of all German nationals from France. He chose to go into exile in Geneva.

Chaplain at Spandau Prison

While at Geneva, Cohen's heard of the plight of the large number of French prisoners being held at Spandau prison, fourteen kilometres outside Berlin. In spite of failing health, he agreed to minister to them and travelled to Berlin in November 1870. The Prussian authorities would not allow a French priest to be appointed chaplain. Spandau prison was

---

24.   The Kensington instrument was erected by the German organ builder, August Friedrich Hermann Gern (1837-1907), who worked for Cavaillé-Coll at the time and who went on to establish his own firm in London later in 1866. Gern was known to build over one hundred instruments in the United Kingdom of which just a handful survive. In 1870, Widor would become organist at the Parisian church of Saint-Sulpice (6th arrondissement) where Cohen had preached. In 1871 Guilmant would become organist of the Church of The Holy Trinity (Église de la Sainte-Trinité), also in Paris (9th arrondissement).

25.   Quoted Tierney, *The Story,* p. 78. Sadly, the church built by Cohen together with its Cavaillé-Coll organ was destroyed by incendiary bombing on 20 February 1944.

26.   As attested to by Dr. Boissarie who noted: "We are not accustomed to cures as complete and instantaneous as this. They are quite outside the rules and traditions of our art. For my part I don't know how to contest or interpret this happening." (Quoted Tierney, *The Story,* p. 92).

packed with over five thousand prisoners living in terrible conditions. Infectious diseases were rampant, including smallpox. Cohen worked tirelessly as a prison chaplain, distributing supplies as well as offering spiritual comfort, no doubt taking the advice he had given to others when he once said: "Always in your conversations, you ought to direct people to God and to God's love and service."[27] He celebrated Mass daily (with a regular congregation of over five hundred prisoners) and celebrated the Sacrament of Reconciliation. Ignoring the advice to administer the Sacrament of the Sick by use of a spatula, Cohen, preferring to use his hands, soon contracted smallpox. He died on 19 January 1871. His remains were interred at Saint Hedwig's Cathedral in Berlin. When the cathedral was destroyed during World War II, they were transferred to the cathedral cemetery. In 2008 the remains of Hermann Cohen were exhumed and brought to the priory in Le Broussey where he had first entered Carmel and where a the community of Discalced friars flourishes today. The cause for the beatification of Venerable Augustine Mary of the Blessed Sacrament (Hermann Cohen), OCD, was introduced in the Diocese of Bordeaux on 19 January 2016.

Music

That Hermann Cohen was a first-rate musician is beyond doubt. Certainly, his talent as a concert pianist is well confirmed by those who knew and heard him. It is more difficult to assess his compositional output. His music has been studied to some extent,[28] but the current scarcity of both live performances and recordings of Cohen's music makes it difficult for most to get to know the Carmelite composer's work.

Cohen's compositional output may be divided into two periods, more or less coinciding with the time before and after his conversion to Christianity.

Piano Works

The first period in Cohen's compositional output is dominated by piano pieces, brilliant and often requiring great virtuosity in performance. He produced a collection of dances for piano entitled *Fleurs d'Hiver* (Flowers of Winter). The collection *Twelve Virtuoso Pieces* was published by the leading Italian music publisher, Ricordi. Cohen's *Reminiscences of I*

---

27.   Tierney, *A Life*, Part II (Writings), p. 324.
28.   Two studies in French are Jean-Marie Beaurin, OSB, *Flèche de Feu* (Paris: Éditions France-Empire, 1982) and Benôit-Marie de l'Éucharisite, OCD, "Hermann Cohen 'interprète de la grâce divine'" in *Éditions du Carmel*, 54, pp. 21-44.

Lombardi recasts themes from the opera, *I Lombardi alla Prima Crociata*, of Giuseppe Verdi (1831-1901) and, like the opera, is Romantic in its aesthetic in recalling the world of the Middle Ages. We noted earlier that from an early age Cohen could memorise music from the world of opera. His teacher Liszt was known for extemporising elaborate opera paraphrases on the piano. Cohen's best-known piano piece, *Les Bords de l'Elbe* (The Banks of the Elbe) is written predominantly in waltz rhythm and wistfully recalls his native Hamburg and its river. Again, in the Romantic vein, he also produced a nocturne for piano entitled *Nuit Vénitienne* (Venetian Night) and a lullaby, *Schlummerlied* (Slumber Song).

Religious Works

The second period of Cohen's compositional output is represented by various collections of religious works:

Many of the texts set to music by Cohen were written by Sister Marie-Pauline du Fougerais, a talented poet and member of the Visitation Order. It is worth noting the impact that Cohen's music had in the United States. His liturgical music was brought there by Carmelite nuns and also by orders of sisters with French roots.

Mass of Saint Teresa of Avila

The 1852 *Mass of Saint Teresa of Avila* was premiered in 1856 in Bordeaux. It was recorded in 1984 by the Carmelite Church Choir at Kensington, with Lynda Richardson (soprano), Leslie Fyson (Baritone), and William Davies (organ), under the direction of the renowned choral conductor, the late John McCarthy (1916-2009). On the same occasion the setting of *Flos Carmeli* from Cohen's third collection, *Fleurs du Carmel*, was also set down along with a *Panis vivus* (Living Bread) in French. Listening to Cohen's *Mass* setting today one is struck by how suitable it is even for use with the modern liturgy. Apart from the setting of the Credo, the parts of the *Mass* are not excessively lengthy. Its memorable melodies, recurring themes and relatively straightforward choral writing make it an approachable work for a competent church choir working with good soloists. Cohen's melody writing and the style of the accompaniment has a distinctly Germanic character to it, in many ways out of the *lied* (or "art song") tradition.

Conclusion

The life of Hermann Cohen is truly fascinating to consider, colourful in its detail, in itself an inspiring spiritual odyssey. He was a brilliant concert pianist, favourite pupil of the great Franz Liszt, who was haunted by an addiction to gambling. He was a convert to Christianity who still liked to refer to himself with humour "as a wandering Jew" when on one of his busy preaching tours. He was personally acquainted with many religious figures of his day, Pope Pius IX, Saint John Vianney (the Curé of Ars), and Saint Bernadette Soubirous. He inspired Blessed Charles de Foucauld. Cohen was a friar, a priest, a founder, a prior, a formator, a hermit, a pilgrim, a missionary, a preacher, a confessor, a prison chaplain, friend, and confidant to many. It is to be hoped that in the future many more can come to know this Carmelite better through his music and, even more, be led through the medium of his art to knowledge of God in adoration, love, and service.

7

Francis Poulenc's *Dialogues des Carmélites*

Known in English simply as "The Carmelites," *Dialogues des Carmélites*, as its French name suggests, is an opera in which words are paramount. It is first and foremost a work of musical dialogue, one in which dramatic detail is kept to a minimum. Nonetheless, this musical drama culminates in one of the most chillingly evocative scenes in modern opera, a scene the sheer emotional intensity of which has left audiences stunned since the work was first performed in 1957. In that final scene, led by their prioress, fourteen Carmelite nuns make their way to the scaffold singing the *Salve Regina*. As each falls beneath the guillotine's blade, the chorus diminishes until only the voice of a novice, Sister Constance, is heard. Suddenly her sister novice, Blanche, who previously had fled in fear, makes her way confidently through the crowd, mounts the scaffold, singing the last four lines of the *Veni Creator*. Her voice is suddenly cut short.

The Carmelite Nuns of Compiègne[1]

At the beginning of the French Revolution in 1789, the community at the Carmel of Compiègne numbered twenty-one sisters: sixteen choir sisters, three lay sisters, and two externs. Mother Thérèse of Saint Augustine, the prioress, had been elected in 1786.

The terrible impact of the Revolution began to be felt among the sisters of Compiègne when their young novice, Sister Constance, was prevented from making her profession on 15 December 1789, on account of a decree by the National Assembly expressly forbidding the pronouncing of religious vows in France. This prohibition on religious profession marked the beginning of a complex chain of events which was to lead to the ultimate demise of the Compiègne community.

On 4 and 5 August 1790, the District Commission of Compiègne arrived at the convent to make an inventory of all its possessions and to interrogate each of the nuns privately as to her intentions. Each of the

---

1. The best extended account of the Carmelites martyred at Compiègne is William Bush, *To Quell The Terror: The Mystery of the Vocation of the Sixteen Carmelites of Compiègne Guillotined July 17, 1774* (Washington DC, ICS Publications: 2013).

sisters expressed her wish to live and die as a Carmelite.

In September 1792, all was finally lost for the Carmelites of Compiègne. All the convent's possessions were confiscated on 12 September, and two days later the nuns themselves were forced to leave. They were obliged to adopt non-religious garb and were no longer permitted to live openly as a community. The sisters split into separate groups and lived at three different addresses near the church of Saint Antoine, where their chaplain, Abbé Courouble, celebrated mass for them.

On 19 September the sisters took the *Liberté-Egalité* oath in order to be able to receive a pension from the revolutionary government. Around this time the prioress proposed an act of consecration whereby the community would offer itself for the ills afflicting the Church. This act of consecration came to be known as the community's "vow of martyrdom."

Arrest

The Carmelites were eventually transferred to Paris's infamous Conciergerie on 13 July 1794, staying there for four days during which they celebrated the feast of Our Lady of Mount Carmel. On that occasion, Sister Julie de Neuville composed a hymn to be sung to the tune of the Marseillaise. The following day the nuns appeared before the Revolutionary Tribunal of Fouquier-Tinville. By all accounts it was hardly a fair trial: there were no lawyers, no witnesses, and no adequate presentation of evidence. The sixteen Carmelites were termed "fanatics" by the Tribunal and condemned to death for counter-revolutionary activities.

The prioress asked the executioner for the right to die last in order to be able to sustain her daughters. She gave each of the sisters a cup of chocolate. The Office of the Dead was sung on the way to the scaffold, together with the *Miserere*, the *Salve Regina,* and the *Te Deum*. Hidden in the crowds, disguised priests blessed the nuns and quietly pronounced the formula of absolution. At the foot of the guillotine, the Carmelites intoned *Veni Creator* and renewed their vows. The first to die was the novice, Sister Constance. Finally, the prioress went to her death with the words "Love will always triumph." Ten days after the execution of the Carmelites the Great Terror ended.

One hundred years later, on the occasion of the centenary of the martyrdom, the Carmelites decided to put forward the cause for beatification. Proceedings began on 28 June 1896 at the request of the Carmel of Compiègne, which had been restored in 1866. Beatification came on

Francis Poulenc was born in January 1899 to a family living in a wealthy section of Paris, France. At the time of his death in 1963, he left a vast legacy of musical compositions: solo piano works, songs, chamber music, sonatas for various instruments, concertos, orchestral works, secular choral works, and a number of stage works.

27 May 1906.

The story of the Carmelite nuns of Compiègne exercised a huge influence on the religious imagination of 19th century France. In September 1896, Monseigneur de Teil spoke on the Compiègne martyrs at the Carmel of Lisieux in the presence of Sister Thérèse of the Child Jesus. For most of her brief life in Carmel, this future saint was much devoted to the memory of the Martyrs of Compiègne.

Francis Poulenc[2]

Francis Poulenc was born on 7 January 1899 at 2 Place des Saussaies, in Paris's affluent eighth arrondissement. The future composer grew up

---

2. For the life and works of Francis Poulenc, see Wilfrid Mellers, *Francis Poulenc* (Oxford: OUP, 1993) and Benjamin Ivry, *Francis Poulenc* (London: Phaidon Press, 1996).

in an extremely cultured environment. Books, works of art, and music abounded. His mother, a very talented pianist, was Francis's first music teacher. A child prodigy, it was not long before his mother decided that she should pass him over to a teacher of greater expertise than herself. Catalan pianist, Ricardo Viñes, became the boy's new teacher. Throughout all this, Francis's mother strove to ensure that his education was unconventional, resisting the suggestions of others that he should follow a more "serious" musical curriculum.

Poulenc's adult life was to be marked by a distinct disregard for convention, and in matters of religion he was something of a contradiction. He once described himself as "Janus-Poulenc," referring to the Roman god who is traditionally shown looking both ways. Even after his apparent "conversion" in the nineteen-thirties, Poulenc managed to maintain within his personality something of the playboy and something of the deeply pious Catholic. Nevertheless, two incidents in the nineteen-thirties led to the more serious aspect of Janus-Poulenc asserting itself.

Firstly, there was a decline in his family fortunes with consequent money problems. Secondly, a close friend of Poulenc's died in an appalling car accident. Mourning for his lost friend inspired Poulenc to write *Litanies à la Vierge Noire de Rocamadour* (1936), his first important religious work. *Litanies* was inspired by the Black Virgin of Rocamadour in southern France, an important place of pilgrimage from medieval times.

From this point on, Poulenc's music tended to alternate between worldly humour and ardent expression of faith; even a number of his religious works have something of the "music hall" about them. His religious inspiration was to reach its highest point in his *Dialogues des Carmélites* (1953-1956). Among other religious works he composed were *Messe* (1937), *Quatre Motets pour un temps de Pénitence* (1938-39), *Exultate Deo* (1941), *Salve Regina* (1941), *Quatre Petites Prières de Saint François d'Assise* (1948), *Stabat Mater* (1950), *Quatre Motets pour un temps de Noël* (19512), *Ave verum corpus* (1952), *Laudes de Saint Antoine de Padoue* (1957-1959), *Gloria* (1959), and, finally, *Sept répons des ténèbres* (1961-1962).

In 1963, six years after the premiere of *Dialogues des Carmélites*, Poulenc died of a massive heart attack in his Paris apartment. Apart from his religious works, Poulenc left a vast legacy of musical compositions: solo piano works, songs, chamber music, sonatas for various instruments, concertos, orchestral works, secular choral works, and a number of stage works. Children of all ages have long delighted in his *Story of Babar, the Little Elephant* (1940-1945).

Dialogues des Carmélites

In 1953 the Italian music publisher Ricordi invited Poulenc to compose a major work for La Scala opera house in Milan. The original idea was for a ballet based on the life of Saint Margaret of Cortona. Poulenc found this theme to be uninspiring and insisted that he would prefer to write an opera. It was at this point that Guido Valcarenghi, director of Ricordi, suggested Georges Bernanos's play *Dialogues des Carmélites* as a possible basis for an operatic work. Bernanos's play was completed just before the Catholic author's death and was intended for a film based on a short novel by the German writer, Gertrud von le Fort, called *Die Letzte am Schafott* ("The Last on the Scaffold"). Von le Fort's work is important in at least one respect: she introduces the fictitious figure of Blanche de la Force for the first time. Bernanos follows Von le Fort very closely as he crafts his own drama. For him, several key themes emerge: the spirit of childhood, poverty, abandonment to Divine Providence, the agony of Christ, the Christian understanding of death and the complementary nature of religious vocation and honour. Overall, Bernanos's work is imbued with a profound sense of peace, serenity and joy.

Poulenc began work on his opera with enthusiasm. There was one problem, however. The American dramatist, Emmet Lavery, had acquired the rights to Gertrud Von le Fort's original novel and had written a stage version in English, *Song at the Scaffold* (1949). This gave rise to complex legal disputes that dogged the two years Poulenc spent writing his opera. The squabble was eventually resolved by means of an agreement that Lavery's name would appear on the programme of every performance of *Dialogues*.

Poulenc became obsessed by his opera. To one friend he wrote, "I have begun *Les Carmélites* and literally cannot sleep because of it!"[3] Later he says, "I am working like a madman, I do not go out, I do not see anyone... I do not want to think of anything else.... I am completing one scene a week. I am crazy about my subject, to the point of believing that I have actually known these women."[4]

One biographer of Poulenc, Benjamin Ivry, gives us an interesting aside as part of his overall treatment of the French composer's *Dialogues*, "Father Griffin, a Carmelite Priest from Dallas, wrote to Poulenc to

3.   Quoted in Mellers, *op. cit.*, p. 103.
4.   *Ibid.*

inquire about the opera's progress. On receiving the composer's reply that God only knew if he would finish it, the priest promised that every Carmelite in the USA would say a novena for Poulenc so that he might complete the work."[5]

From the outset, Poulenc was concerned to emphasise the *words* of his opera. He always held the view that his opera should be performed in the language of a particular audience. Nowadays his work is most often performed in French, but its first performance was in Italian, and the English version was first performed shortly afterwards. Throughout his opera, Poulenc is at pains to ensure the audience can follow the *libretto* without difficulty. To his friend and confidant, Pierre Bernac, he wrote, "It just flows and flows, and it is like nobody but myself. It is madly vocal. I check each note and am careful to place the right vowels on the high notes. Not to mention the prosody: I do believe that every word will be understood."[6]

The composition process was further complicated by a Poulenc's profound sense of personal tragedy. "Black butterflies are still flying around me," he says at one point.[7] His companion of several years, Lucien Roubert, was seriously ill during the period of the composition of *Dialogues*. By strange coincidence Roubert died on the very evening Poulenc completed the opera in August 1955: "I got up from my table and said to faithful Anna [his cook], 'I have finished: Monsieur Lucien will die now.'"[8]

The music of Poulenc's *Dialogues des Carmélites* is in keeping with the grandeur and austerity of the text with which he worked. He was, of course, a master songwriter. The melodic line of his opera constantly brings out the best in each voice. He scores the work for a very large orchestra but always orchestrates discretely, never allowing the words to be overpowered by the music. Above all, there are no grand arias. Poulenc's *Dialogues* is a true example of art that conceals art. There is nothing mawkish, sentimental or overblown about Poulenc's masterpiece. On the printed score the epigraph quotes from Saint Teresa of Avila, "God keep me from gloomy Saints."

Dialogues des Carmélites was performed for the first time at La Scala on 26 January 1957; the Paris premiere took place on 21 June of the same year. The first performance in English was at Covent Garden, London,

---

5. Ivry, *op. cit.*, p. 174. Unfortunately, Ivry gives us no further information regarding the identity of Fr Griffin. Neither does he provide a source for his information.
6. Quoted in Mellers, *op. cit.*, p. 103.
7. Quoted in Ivry, *op. cit.*, p. 178.
8. Quoted in Mellers, *op. cit.*, pp. 103-4.

on 16 January 1958 (previously a performance, in French, had taken place at San Francisco Opera in September 1957).

Synopsis

ACT ONE

Scene One, April 1789. The Paris Mansion of the Marquis de la Force: The opera opens in the library of the Marquis de la Force. The marquis is concerned at the failure of his daughter Blanche to return home. The French Revolution is at its height, and her carriage has got caught up in the crowd. Blanche, an extremely nervous young woman, eventually makes her way home. The girl is very jumpy and is terrified even by the mere shadow of a servant cast on the wall of her home. Blanche declares that it is her intention to become a Carmelite nun and hopes that she will find some respite from her fear in the isolation of the cloister.

Scene Two, The Parlour of the Carmelite Convent in Compiègne: The action moves to the Carmel of Compiègne. Blanche asks the prioress, Madame de Croissy, an old woman and obviously ill, to accept her into the Order. The prioress is slightly concerned that Blanche's only motive is to flee from the world. She relents only when Blanche tells her of her intention to adopt the name *Soeur Blanche de l'Agonie du Christ*.

Scene Three, The Inside of the Convent: We are introduced to the cheerful novice, Sister Constance, who shares the household chores with Blanche. Constance expresses her willingness to offer God her own life to save that of the dying prioress. Blanche is unnerved and expresses her own fear of death.

Interlude (Orchestra)

Scene Four, The Cell of the Infirmary: the dying prioress has a vision of the destruction of the cloister. She is troubled by Blanche's instability and commends her to the care of Mother Marie of the Incarnation. The prioress battles with her own fear of death and with religious doubt.

Act Two

Scene One, The Chapel at Night: The prioress has died, and Blanche is presented, once again, in turmoil. Mother Marie of the Incarnation upbraids her and sends her to her cell to calm down.

Interlude before the Curtain: Sister Constance declares her wish that Mother Marie will become the new prioress. While she muses on the

Painting capturing the Carmelite nuns of Compiègne as they were put to death by the French Revolutionary government because of refusal to refute their religious profession. The story of the martyrdom of the Compiègne community is the subject of Poulenc's *Dialogues des Carmélites*.

death of the old prioress, she comes to realise that she may have died someone else's death. Each person dies for others, she concludes.

Scene Two, The Hall of the Chapter House: The election for a new prioress takes place in the chapter house. Mother Marie is not chosen. The new prioress is Mother Lidoine. The visit of Blanche's brother, the Chevalier de la Force, is announced. The Chevalier wishes to say farewell to his sister before he emigrates. The new prioress instructs Mother Marie to listen in on the conversation.

Scene Three, The Parlour of the Convent: The Chevalier de la Force urges his sister to return to her father. Blanche rejects his advice, claiming to have overcome her fear within the cloister. Her brother is not pleased and turns to go, leaving a distraught Blanche behind.

Scene Four, The Sacristy: The chaplain bids farewell to the nuns. He has been stripped of his post by the revolutionaries. Commissioners announce the decree dissolving the cloister. Blanche, overcome by fear, drops a statuette of the Child Jesus she has been clutching for comfort. It smashes to pieces on the floor.

ACT THREE

Scene One, The Chapel: In the ruined chapel of the cloister, the nuns have come together with their confessor. In the absence of the prioress, Mother Marie calls on her sisters to take an oath of martyrdom to preserve the Carmelite Order, but insists that the oath must be unanimous. Initially, Constance is unwilling to comply but later changes her mind. As the confessor begins his words of blessing over each of the sisters, Blanche flees.

Interlude before the Curtain: The new prioress, who was not present for the oath of martyrdom, expresses her concern to avoid any action which might endanger the lives of her nuns.

Scene Two, The Library of the Marquis de la Force: Blanche flees to the plundered house of her father, whom the revolutionaries have executed. Mother Marie tries to give her an address where she can find safe refuge, but Blanche wants to stay in the house disguised as a servant girl.

Interlude (Orchestra): Blanche learns of the arrest of the Carmelites.

Scene Three, A Cell in the Conciergerie: In prison, the prioress seeks to boost her sisters' morale. Constance is sure that Blanche will return. A revolutionary commissioner reads aloud the nuns' death sentence.

Interlude before the curtain: Mother Marie wants to die with the sisters, but the confessor forbids her to go to the prison.

Scene Four, The Place de la Conciergerie: A huge crowd has gathered in the square where the execution is about to take place. Led to the scaffold by the prioress, the nuns sing *Salve Regina* as they ascend. Constance is the last to die. On her way to the scaffold, she sees Blanche coming through the crowd. Blanche, too, goes to her death, with the last verse to of the *Veni Creator* on her lips. She has overcome her fear.

Musical Highlights

Opening Music

The opening bars of *Dialogues des Carmélites* are extremely impressive. Poulenc is obviously inspired by the classical French overture, and his take on this traditional form is in keeping with the grandiose setting of the house of the Marquis de la Force. At the same time, however, the music, while it looks to the past, does bring with it a sense of impending doom.

Act One, Scene Four

The death scene of the first prioress is one of the greatest moments in modern opera. The emotional level borders on the hysterical and has much in common with traditional Italian opera. There is, however, a constant sense of dignity and control even when things are at their most tense. The prioress's vocal part is marked *très rude*. Poulenc's intention is to contrast the horror of the scene with the serenity with which Blanche faces her death at the end of the opera. The score is marked with comments about the prioress's death rattle. The overall effect is macabre.

Act Two, Scene Two

The second prioress's monologue shows off the dramatic soprano's voice to great advantage. The vocal part is extremely rich and has long been regarded as a masterly bringing together of words and music.

Act Two, Scene Three

An opera about the martyrdom of Carmelite nuns hardly lends itself to the kind of love duets common in many operas. Nevertheless, Blanche's duet with her brother, the Chevalier de la Force, is the closest we come to "love" music. There is an incredible warmth and tenderness in the Chevalier's part, particularly when he sings about his sister. The tenor is encouraged by the score to sing in the open-throated style of Italian opera. It is hardly surprising that this duet won sustained applause during the opera's first performance at La Scala, Milan.

Act Three, Interlude

The interlude in Act Three of *Dialogues* is a work of real innovation. Spoken dialogue is accompanied by the inventive use of percussion: tom-tom and wood block. This unusual ensemble accompanies the news of the arrest of the Carmelite nuns. Commentators would suggest that Poulenc's music is consciously suggestive of certain kinds of physical torture.

Act Three, Scene Four

The most famous scene in Poulenc's opera is that of the execution. The composer's musical imitation of the sound of the guillotine's falling blade is terrifyingly realistic.

Conclusion

Words can only achieve a certain amount when it comes to describing music. It is to be hoped that readers may have the opportunity of seeing and hearing Poulenc's masterpiece for themselves. The French composer's work is profoundly Carmelite in ways which go beyond his merely having chosen a Carmelite theme. Poulenc heeds Saint Teresa's warning about holiness and gloominess; his opera is tense, but never gloomy. Furthermore, Blanche's confident abandonment at the close of the opera puts us very much in mind of the "little way" of confidence and abandonment of Saint Thérèse of Lisieux, a way which can achieve great things through a radical acceptance of our littleness before God. Since classical times the test of all good drama is the extent to which it is *catharsis* (purgation or purification) for the audience. Francis Poulenc's masterpiece, *Dialogues des Carmélites*, is indeed cathartic. The audience cannot help but be caught up in the journey of faith of young Blanche, a journey from darkness into light, from fear into hope, from timidity into courageous abandonment to Divine Love.

◊ ◊ ◊

8

Sir Lennox Berkeley's
Four Poems by St. Teresa of Avila

Lennox Berkeley: Life and Works[1]

Lennox Randal Francis Berkeley was born into an aristocratic family on 12 May 1903 at Sunningwell Plains, Boars Hill, near Oxford, England. Today Boars Hill has a strong Carmelite connection being the location of a community of Discalced friars, the famous *Carmelite Book Service*, and the editorial headquarters of *Mount Carmel* review. Lennox's grandmother, Cécile, was of French and Scottish origin, her family being the Counts Drummond de Melfort. Berkeley's father was a British naval officer, his mother being the daughter of the British consul for Monaco.

After initial schooling at the Dragon School, Oxford, the young Lennox was educated at Gresham's School in Holt, Norfolk (where he was followed as a student by the poet W.H. Auden and the composer Benjamin Britten), at Saint George's School in Harpenden, Hertfordshire, and at Merton College, Oxford. He graduated in 1926 with a degree in French. Lennox did not reveal a particular talent for music while at school, although contemporaries remember his rather florid way of playing the piano. However, as a student at Oxford, he began to compose in earnest and had a number of his early works performed.

On account of his ancestry, Berkeley always had strong affinities with France and was a close friend of leading French composers of his day, Maurice Ravel and Francis Poulenc. On Ravel's advice, Berkeley took lessons with Nadia Boulanger. Boulanger was a legendary teacher who counted many world-famous composers and performers among her pupils, including Aaron Copland, John Eliot Gardiner, Philip Glass, and Astor Piazzolla. Classes with her were notoriously demanding: as encouraging as she was of genuine talent, she reduced the young Berkeley to tears on occasion due to the high technical standards she demanded.

---

1. For the life and works of Lennox Berkeley, see Peter Dickinson, *The Music of Lennox Berkeley*, 2nd edition (Woodbridge, Suffolk and Rochester, NY: The Boydell Press, 2003). See also the substantial entries on Berkeley and his music at *Oxford Dictionary of National Biography* (online) and *Grove Music* (online).

Berkeley stayed with Boulanger for six years and remained grateful for her teaching for the rest of his life: as with so many of her students, Boulanger (one of whose mottoes was "without discipline there is no freedom") enabled him to find his own "voice" as a composer. Berkeley had works performed in Paris, and the BBC broadcast his oratorio, *Jonah*, in 1935.

Over the course of a long career, Berkeley went on to compose in every genre, producing symphonies, concertos, oratorios, operas, works for strings, songs, chamber music, and music for a variety of solo instruments. He also composed extensively for both the Roman Catholic and Anglican liturgy. He was of the same generation as composers Sir William Walton and Sir Michael Tippett (and Benjamin Britten remained a close life-long friend) but Berkeley's own music "spoke" with a definite French accent, somewhat different to that of the traditions established by earlier composers in Britain such as Sir Edward Elgar and Ralph Vaughan Williams.

From 1946 to 1968 Berkeley was Professor of Composition at the Royal Academy of Music. A deeply committed Roman Catholic, Berkeley had a Papal Knighthood of the Order of Saint Gregory bestowed upon him in 1973. The following year he was knighted by Queen Elizabeth II. Berkeley died at London on 26 December 1989, and his funeral took place at Westminster Cathedral. He was survived by his wife, Freda, and their three sons, the eldest of whom, Michael, is a major composer in Britain today.

Berkeley's Religious Faith

Berkeley converted to Roman Catholicism in 1928, two years after his graduation from Oxford and during his period of study with Boulanger in Paris. In a radio talk Berkeley (whose own father interestingly had published a work entitled *Mysticism and Mathematics*) spoke of music as belonging first and foremost to the spiritual world:

Music does not speak to the intellect alone. Its most important contact with the listener is of another order for it belongs first and foremost to the spiritual world and the best music is that which communicates the most strongly and the most urgently on that level.[2]

The composer Malcolm Williamson went so far as to suggest that every work Berkeley ever wrote was religious and, whatever the subject, Berkeley was a religious composer "who could conceive of life in no terms

---

2. Quoted in Peter Dickinson, *op. cit.*, p. 101.

Lennox Randal Francis Berkeley was born into an aristocratic family in 1903 at Boars Hill, near Oxford, England, an area with a strong Carmelite connection. He died in 1989.

other than religious music."[3] Sir John Tavener (see Chapter 9), a former student of Berkeley, stated:

> It is impossible to manufacture true "devotional" music and it seems to me that Lennox Berkeley's greatest music is his religious music. The most important things about a person are usually the least easily described: Lennox's expression, for instance, when, unknown to him, I have seen him after Mass in Westminster Cathedral.[4]

3. *Ibid.*
4. *Ibid.*

Saint Teresa of Avila as Poet[5]

In her lifetime, Saint Teresa was known as a "maker of verses," writing hymns, rhymes, shepherd songs, and poems of love. In Chapter 16 (4) of her autobiography, she describes herself as one "who though not a poet suddenly composed some deeply-felt verses well expressing her pain."[6] It would seem that Saint Teresa composed many verses in her life-time, about thirty of those which survive are recognised to be genuine. In recent years autograph copies of some the poems have come to light.Saint Teresa's verses would seem to have been written following on experience in prayer or to mark a feast day or day of special celebration. Her poems often had their origins in song: a pre-existing melody or rhythm could inspire Saint Teresa to compose new words. Saint Teresa had an innate musicality, and her poems were innately musical. Those proficient in the Spanish language readily attest to the fact that Saint Teresa's poems were meant to be sung. It is common in performances today to hear her poems sung in Spanish accompanied by guitar or other stringed instruments, often with simple percussion instruments.

Berkeley's *Four Poems by Saint Teresa of Avila*[7]

Lennox Berkeley composed his *Four Poems by Saint Teresa of Avila* (Opus 27) in 1947 just before completing his *Piano Concerto* (Opus 29). The cycle was first broadcast in April 1948 on BBC Radio and sung by much loved English *contralto*, Kathleen Ferrier.[8] This period also saw the composition of Berkeley's other important religious work, *Stabat mater* (Opus 28).

Although Berkeley has strong affinities with French music, the *Four*

---

5.   The story of the life of Saint Teresa of Jesus (of Avila) is so well known it is not told here.The focus here is on her poetry. See Eugene McCaffrey, OCD, *Introduction to the Writings of Saint Teresa of Avila* (Dublin and Manchester: Carmelite Centre of Spirituality and Koinonia, 1981).Also Eugene McCaffrey, OCD, *The Writings of Saint Teresa of Avila: An Introduction* (Boars Hill, Oxford: Teresian Press, 2014). Also the "Introduction" to Saint Teresa's Poetry in Kieran Kavanaugh, OCD and Otilio Rodriguez, OCD, transl., *The Collected Works of Saint Teresa of Avila*, vol. III. (Washington, DC: ICS Publications, 1985).

6.   Saint Teresa of Jesus (of Avila), *The Book of Her Life* (16.4) in Kieran Kavanaugh, OCD and Otilio Rodriguez, OCD, transl., *The Collected Works of Saint Teresa of Avila*, vol. I., 2nd edition (Washington, DC: ICS Publications, 1987), p. 149.

7.   For a musical analysis of Berkeley's *Four Poems by Saint Teresa of Avila*, see Peter Dickinson, *op. cit.*, pp. 101-114.

8.   The poems were recorded by Pamela Bowden (1960, Warner Classics), by Irish singer, Bernadette Greevy (1970's, Irish Recording Company, out of print), and by Catherine Wyn-Rogers (2004, Chandos Records) and are widely available in CD format as well as from the various downloading and streaming services available to listeners today. The recording on the Chandos label has the advantage of reproducing in an accompanying booklet (with the permission of his estate) the texts of the Saint Teresa's poems in Symons's translation (as used by Berkeley); the booklet may be downloaded at the Chandos website in PDF.

Poems by Saint Teresa of Avila are a fine example of the tradition of English writing for strings. At times there is some solo writing for violin or cello, sounding out against the background of the rest of the strings. Sometimes Berkeley divides up the string voices, beyond the standard four parts in order to enrich the harmonies, adding new touches of tone colour; in this kind of impressionism, the English and the French elements of Berkeley's musical imagination come together. Berkeley's *Four Poems by Saint Teresa of Avila* are excellent examples of what would be called "art song" in classical music, but both the words and the music have their roots in dance, in folk rhythm, folk melody, lullaby, and lament.

The Texts[9]

As is so often the case, much is lost in the translation of Saint Teresa's Spanish poetry into English. Accurate modern translations keep us close to the original meaning, and in recent times some English translations have sought to retain the musicality of the original.[10] It is undoubtedly the case that the particular translations of the poetry of Saint Teresa by the leading English poet Arthur William Symons (1865-1945), which Berkeley chose as his text, read as better poetry in English (in terms of rhyme and rhythm and overall "musicality") and lent themselves ideally to being set by Berkeley. Symons, who was himself heavily influenced by the French "symbolist" poets Charles Baudelaire and Paul Verlaine, exerted an important influence on both W.B. Yeats and T.S. Eliot. Three of the poems set by Berkeley (nos. 1, 2, and 4) are authentic poems of Saint Teresa. Perhaps somewhat disappointingly, the finest in the complete set, no. 3, is not by Saint Teresa herself but was (as we shall see) the text of a popular song which was nonetheless very dear to her; both the composer, Berkeley, and his lyricist, Symons, would have understood Saint Teresa to be the author of all four poems.

First poem: "If, Lord, Thy love for me is strong" (no. 4, Loving Colloquy, *Si el amor que me tenéis*)

The first poem is an intensely felt dialogue with God, employing a rather anguished musical theme. Truthfully, on first listening, it is per-

---

9.   The numbering of the poems below follows the standard Kavanaugh-Rodriguez English edition, *op. cit.*, vol. III (the poetry was translated by Fr Adrian Cooney, OCD, based on the Tomás Alvarez Spanish edition of 1977), from which edition the titles are also taken. As stated above, the third poem set by Berkeley was not by Saint Teresa. The first line of the original Spanish is given in each case.

10.   Eric W. Vogt, *The Complete Poetry of Saint Teresa of Avila: A Bilingual Edition* (New Orleans, LA: University Press of the South, 1996) is recommended.

Saint Teresa of Avila was known for writing hymns, rhymes, shepherd songs, and poems of love, some thirty of those which survive are recognised to be genuine. She had an innate musicality, and her poems were innately musical.

haps the least attractive number in the set. This is partly because of its conflicted subject matter, namely an intense desire for God seeking to co-exist with a sense of frustration at God's apparent distance: "If, Lord, Thy love for me is strong/As this which binds me unto Thee/What holds me from Thee, Lord, so long/What holds Thee, Lord, so long from me?" As a consequence, there are strong clashes in the music and a certain mixture of bitter and sweet in the harmonies employed by Berkeley. The composer rewrote the music for the phrase "What holds Thee, Lord, so long from me?" after the first performance, giving "Lord" a new dramatic high note (to be sung *fortissimo*) and directing the singer to slow down for emphasis. The somewhat contentious mood of this first piece is soon to be dispelled by what follows.

Second poem: "Shepherd, shepherd, hark that calling!" (no. 14, At the Birth of the Infant God, *Mi gallejo, mira quién llama*)

The second poem is a Christmas pastoral, set among shepherds on the occasion of the birth of the infant Jesus. Its use of a continuous note as a kind of drone, puts the listener very much in mind of bagpipes. The intervals (i.e. the distances between notes) employed by Berkeley are reminiscent of folk music as is some of the writing for solo violin which sounds akin to traditional fiddle playing. The scoring is highly atmospheric and manages to create the effect of light and freshness of air. The whole reminds the experienced listener somewhat of the composer Gustav Mahler when he wrote in a pastoral idiom. It is dawn, and the shepherds in the fields seem to hear the voices of angels (the beating of whose wings can also be heard in the music): "Shepherd, shepherd, hark that calling! Angels they are, and the day is dawning."

Third poem: "Let mine eyes see Thee" (popular song, *Veante mis ojos*)

It is perhaps a pity that the most exquisitely intense musical setting at the heart of the set uses a text not original to Saint Teresa herself. However, it turns out to have been a popular song which was very much enjoyed by her, was close to her spirituality and a major source of inspiration for the Carmelite mystic. On one occasion the singing of it during community recreation by a young novice, Isabel de Jesús, sent Saint Teresa into ecstasy. It was Easter 1571, in Salamanca. The song was a popular one about longing love: "*Veante mis ojos/dulce Jesús bueno./ veante mis ojos/muerame yo luego.*" (Let my eyes see you/O sweet, gentle Jesus./Let my eyes see you/and I will die at once.)[11] These words are immediately recognisable as those set by Berkeley as the third of the poems of Saint Teresa. In her *Meditations on the Song of Songs* (7.2) Saint Teresa elaborates on her experience on hearing the song:

---

11.   See Kieran Kavanaugh, OCD and Carol Lisi, OCDS, eds., Kieran Kavanaugh, OCD and Otilio Rodriguez, transl., Saint Teresa of Avila, *The Interior Castle: Study Edition* (Washington, DC: ICS Publications, 2010), p. 380.

Don't think, daughters, there is any exaggeration in saying that she
dies. As I have said, it indeed happens that love sometimes operates
with such force that it rules over all the powers of the natural subject.
Thus, I know a person [St Teresa herself] who while in this kind of
prayer heard someone, with a beautiful voice, singing; and she certifies
that, in her opinion, if the singing had not stopped the soul would
have gone out of itself on account of the great delight and sweetness
the Lord gave it to enjoy. His Majesty provided that the singing stop,
for the one who was in this suspension could easily have died.[12]

Michael Berkeley, the composer's son, came to know his father's *Four
Poems by Saint Teresa of Avila* while a student at the Royal Academy of
Music where he conducted a performance of the work. He was deeply
moved by his father's setting of this third poem as "just a perfect little
piece of music. It perhaps brought from him some of the strongest emo-
tions– the sacred went straight to his heart and the music came straight
back out again."[13] Michael Berkeley recalled how his father felt this third
song was sometimes sung too slowly and too romantically in performance. The recurrence of the word "death" at the end of various phrases
may sound excessively lugubrious (especially in some performances), but
the music constantly seeks to lift the spirit of the listener. "Death" is the
final word sung by the solo singer, but death does not have the final say.
The exquisite string music which concludes the song is a vision of transformation and Resurrection, with a comforting, rocking motion, almost
like that of a lullaby, leading to a resolution that gives the impression of
a new dawn in a way which draws listeners beyond themselves. This is
a fine example of music having its effect *per aures ad animum* ("through
the ears to the soul"), as an ancient Latin saying puts it.

Fourth poem: "Today a shepherd and our kin" (no. 12, At the Birth of
Jesus, *Hoy nos viene a redimir*)

The fourth poem, although written by Berkeley for voice and string
orchestra, reminds the listener somewhat of one of the organ works of
Johann Sebastian Bach or his contemporaries. There is a singing "hymn-
like" melody with busy notes running around it and a good, solid, driving bass line. Although the subject matter appears similar to that of the
second poem (which also has shepherds and is written in celebration of
the birth of Jesus), there is little of the earlier, light pastoral quality here.
The whole piece has immense swagger and a spirit of bold confidence

12.   Saint Teresa of Jesus (of Avila), *Meditations on the Song of Songs* (7.2), in Kieran Kavanaugh,
OCD and Otilio Rodriguez, OCD, transl., *The Collected Works of Saint Teresa of Avila*, vol. II (Washington, DC: ICS Publications, 1980).
13.   Quoted in Peter Dickinson, *op. cit.*, p. 101.

engendered by its subject matter, the mystery of the Incarnation: "Give over idle parleying… For He is God omnipotent!" The air of assurance and celebration is heightened by Berkeley's continuous use of little fanfare motifs throughout the music.

Conclusion

Sir Lennox Berkeley's musical setting of *Four Poems by St Teresa of Avila* deserves to be better known among music lovers and spiritual pilgrims alike. Listening to the set is in itself an opportunity to appreciate the work of one of England's leading religious composers as well as the lyrical output of one the great mystics of the Christian tradition, to be inspired by composer and poet alike, to consideration of God and his love for us.

9

Sir John Tavener's
Little Requiem for Father Malachy Lynch

Things Remarkable

The funeral of Fr. Malachy Lynch at Aylesford Priory in Kent was by all accounts a remarkable event and not just because it commemorated a truly remarkable man. The occasion was one which drew people from all over, from all walks of life, a testament to the drawing power the man exerted throughout his life. The breath of association was indeed remarkable. Finally, the open-air funeral mass itself was remarkable because of the dramatic intervention of a thunderstorm. A remarkable man, a remarkable life, and a remarkable *requiem*!

At Aylesford Priory, and also at Allington Castle, Fr. Malachy Lynch sought to encourage artists, poets, writers, and musicians. He hosted seminars which fostered cultural exchange and cultural debate. Somehow he saw such expression and exchange to be in continuity with the living tradition of Carmel which he sought to rediscover, to foster, and to live.

One of those musicians who attended the funeral of Fr. Malachy was the English composer, Sir John Tavener, known today to millions for his intensely moving *Song for Athene* (or "Flight of Angels") which accompanied the coffin of Diana, Princess of Wales, as it emerged from the great doors of Westminster Abbey at the end of her funeral service into a sea of mourners outside. In his younger days, Tavener was a friend of Malachy Lynch and was much moved by the experience of attending his funeral in 1972 and, as an artist, much inspired by the dramatic intervention of the thunder storm which raged during the funeral Mass itself. In his autobiography he tells of the genesis of his *Little Requiem for Father Malachy Lynch*:

> At this funeral, an open-air funeral in Aylesford Priory, the idea of the first section of the *Requiem* had already come to me. As I walked away and drove home to London the music began to unfold in my head. This has happened to me on a number of occasions since, where music appears to be given as a parting gift from the dead person.[1]

1. John Tavener, *The Music of Silence – A Composer's Testament* (London: Faber and Faber, 2000),

Fr Malachy Lynch, O. Carm.[2]

William Lynch was born in 1899 in County Wicklow in the Southeast of Ireland. He received his education locally before going to Dublin to attend the Carmelite school there, Terenure College. He entered the noviciate of the Irish Province of Carmelites, taking the religious name Malachy, made simple and then final profession of vows and was ordained to the priesthood in 1925. Following his ordination he went to what was then known as the "English Mission," taking up residence at Faversham in Kent in 1926. At the same time, Fr. James Cogan went to Sittingbourne (also in Kent). In this way, Fr. Malachy Lynch and Fr.   James Cogan were in a real sense the "founding fathers" of the revival of the Carmelite Order in Britain. By the end of the decade, however, Fr. Malachy was recalled to Ireland to become master of novices at Kinsale. In later years one of his former novices, Fr. Anselm Corbett, recalled his formator with great affection: "Fr. Malachy tried to enthuse everybody about what he regarded as divinely inspired lovely things."[3] Evidently, this included music, literature, the Latin language, and Gregorian chant.In the mid 1930's Fr. Malachy was asked to go to Wales, where in Aberystwyth he re-established the Junior Seminary of the Diocese but made sure to incorporate into it boys and young men who were interested not only in training for the priesthood for the Diocese of Menevia (the local diocese) but also those who were interested in joining the Order of Carmelites.

Later Fr. Malachy worked at Lampeter, building a beautiful church there. In 1946 he went further south to Llandilo and then, in 1949, he was appointed to Aylesford where the Carmelites had returned to their medieval foundation. Fr. Malachy was installed as prior there by his brother Kilian, Prior General of the Order. Fr. Malachy worked tirelessly in the restoration of Aylesford Priory, adorning it with many works of art. He did the same at Allington Castle.

The following are the words of Fr. Malachy's obituary in *The Tablet*, penned by his Carmelite confrere Fr. Wilfrid McGreal:

> Fr. Malachy Lynch's death last Friday will be felt as a personal loss by many... He tried to communicate what he believed to be the hallmark of the Carmelite Order, the prophetic vision– the vision epitomised in the life of the prophet Elijah, the spiritual father of Carmel, and

p. 28
    2.   For the life of Fr Malachy Lynch, O. Carm., see Wilfrid McGreal, O. Carm., *A Stumbling Pilgrim Guided by Indirections: A Biography of Carmelite Friar Fr Malachy Lynch, 1899-1972* (Faversham: Saint Albert's Press, 2016).
    3.   Quoted in Fintan Burke, O. Carm., "Homily preached by the Prior Provincial, F. Burke, O. Carm., at the Requiem Mass [for Fr Anselm Corbett, O. Carm.] in Terenure College on 14 June, 2004," www.carmelites.ie.

John Tavener was born in 1944 at Wembley Park, in North London, a direct descendant of the sixteenth-century composer John Taverner. He befriended Carmelite Father Malachy Lynch and was deeply impressed by him. Inspired during Fr. Malachy's open-air funeral Tavener later composed his *Little Requiem for Father Malachy Lynch*.

of course Mary's faith. It was this prayerful vision that gave Malachy his wonderful gift of language, whether written as in the Newsletter or those thousands of sermons he preached at Aylesford. The vision was also that of the artist: an artist who inspired people to create, and in this way gave scope to such distinguished artists as Philip Lindsay, Michael Clark, Adam Kossowski, and Moira Forsyth. The vision also expressed itself in his ability to communicate to those in need.[4]

Fr. Edward Maguire's homily at Fr. Malachy's funeral mass describes a man, who was clearly larger than life, in vivid terms:

What manner of man was Father Malachy? I would think a combina-

4.   Wilfrid McGreal, in *The Tablet*, 13 May 1972; quoted in Bulletin, *Our Lady of the Assumption Carmelite Province, England and Wales*, June 1972, 3, no. 3, p. 2.

tion of a medieval mystic and a Renaissance prince, with all the vision and the conviction of the former and all the singlemindedness, drive, and determination of the latter – a formidable combination indeed. He met difficulties, tremendous difficulties in the task of building up Aylesford, the task of fulfilling his vision, but they never daunted him. He was in a sense, although helped and supported by many, the driving force, he was the bows that cleaved the waves, he was the engine room that drove things on. If you asked him whose hand was at the helm he would not say it was his at all. He would have said it was Our Lady's. He saw himself as the instrument of Our Lady, the instrument of God.[5]

Fr. Maguire's homily also gives witness to the long-established wisdom that creativity and conviction can be difficult to live with. In this regard he quoted W. B. Yeats: "It was W. B. Yeats, also something of an Irish mystic, who said in his poem *The Second Coming* 'the best lack all conviction while the worst are full of passionate intensity.'" Fr. Maguire went on to say:

He was… a true Carmelite. He was a great lover of Our Lady and a great lover of the brethren, despite the fact that he was not exactly the easiest man to live with. How could a visionary like him be easy to live with? Visionaries are not meant to be easy. They disturb the complacency, routine, the mediocrity of life and we don't like to be pushed into things we are not clear about. No wonder at times that provincials, I am speaking of past provincials, no wonder at times that provincials retired baffled and members of communities were sometimes dazzled and bewildered by the vision that he was following. Nevertheless he brought them along with him.[6]

The homily concludes colourfully:

Yes, the news that he had died last Friday evening cast a shadow. As one of his poet friends said: "It is as if half a world of worth were disappearing over the horizon with the inexorable motion of a great departing ship.[7]

Sir John Tavener[8]

Sir John Tavener was born on 28 January 1944 at Wembley Park, in North London, and was a direct descendant of the sixteenth-century composer John Taverner (note the slight difference in the spelling of the name). The young Tavener attended Highgate School as a music

---

5. *Bulletin*, June 1972, 3, no. 3, p. 2.
6. *Ibid.*, p. 3.
7. *Ibid.*, p. 4.
8. For the life of John Tavener, see John Tavener, *op. cit.*

scholar, a school where the famous and immensely popular composer of religious music, John Rutter (b. 1945), was a fellow student. Eventually enrolling at the Royal Academy of Music in London, Tavener's teachers included Sir Lennox Berkeley (1903-1989), himself associated with Carmel and its spirituality through his exquisite settings of *Four Poems by Saint Teresa of Avila* which were first performed in 1948 in a BBC broadcast by the world-famous contralto, Kathleen Ferrier (see Chapter 8). Early in his career, Tavener followed in his father's footsteps, from the age of fifteen serving as organist at Saint James's Presbyterian Church, Kensington. His first success came in 1968 with the *"dramatic cantata"* *The Whale*. The following year his *Celtic Requiem* was recorded on the famous Apple label, which had been founded by The Beatles; Tavener's brother, a builder, was working for Ringo Starr at the time.

Over his lifetime Tavener became one of the most significant and most loved among the choral composers in Britain. His music often took its inspiration from poetry: from the poets of the English metaphysical tradition, John Donne and Henry Vaughan, but also from the sonnets of William Shakespeare, from the poems of Saint John of the Cross, from the works of the visionary poet and painter, William Blake, and the Irish poet, W.B. Yeats. A longtime member of the Russian Orthodox Church (he converted to Orthodoxy in his thirties), Tavener often drew inspiration from texts of the world's great religions: from Judaism, Islam, Hinduism, and Buddhism. Belonging to the Orthodox Tradition in Eastern Christianity, Tavener regarded his own compositions as "icons in sound." And yet, resonating deeply with the Carmelite tradition, silence was of great importance to him: his autobiography was entitled *The Music of Silence*, and one of his last great musical works was *Towards Silence*. Taking a spiritual reading of our times, Tavener reflected:

> We seem to have lost our contact with the primordial: the idea of—call it divine revelation as opposed to something that's learned by the human intellect—something that, if you lay yourself completely open, and you just open your heart completely, something will actually come into it.[9]

Silence was key to developing this spiritual openness, for Tavener: his music is sound, but it is born of silence and leads towards silence, "speaking" in and to the heart of composer and listener alike. On the occasion of his death on 12 November 2013, speaking to the BBC, his contemporary and fellow composer, John Rutter, remarked that Tavener had the "very rare gift" of being able to "bring an audience to a deep silence. He believed music was for everybody and was a prayer."

---

9.   Interview with journalist, David D'Arcy, on NPR's *Morning Edition*, 8 July 1999.

The Friars, Aylesford in Kent, England, and the reconstructed ancient home of the Carmelites. The major restoration was led by Fr. Malachy Lynch who befriended Tavener.

Sir John and Fr. Malachy

John Tavener first met Fr. Malachy Lynch as a boy, and the Carmelite made an immense impression on him. In his autobiographical work, *The Music of Silence: A Composer's Testament*, Tavener writes:

> The growing preoccupation with finding a way to express metaphysical concepts through musical means had really begun at the time when I first met Father Malachy, when I was twelve. He was one of the most interesting Roman Catholics I have ever met. He was in contact with Sufis and he used to invite Sufis and Methodists down to the ancient castle in Kent where he lived his last years. It was there that I first met Metropolitan Anthony from the Orthodox Church.[10]

The "ancient castle" mentioned is, of course, Allington Castle. Tavener considered Fr. Malachy to be quintessentially Irish as well as something of a Romantic medievalist:

> Father Malachy was an extraordinary man, very Irish, with all the vagueness of the Irish. But the whole idea of tradition was important to him. All around the castle he had little notices encouraging us to keep alive the medieval spirit in art, and he spoke to me a lot about that kind of thing, so it was not surprising that the *Little Requiem for Father Malachy Lynch* (1972) came to me fully born; the first time this

---

10.   John Tavener, *op. cit.*, pp. 27-28.

happened to me.[11]

It would seem that Fr. Malachy Lynch inspired (at least in part) the composition of Tavener's major opera, *Thérèse*, which was based on the life of Saint Thérèse of Lisieux:

> After Father Malachy's death, I felt that I wanted to write an opera based on Saint Thérèse of Lisieux; this intense twenty-four-year-old saint who appears to do nothing at all during her earthly existence.[12]

Tavener's completed opera was premiered at the Royal Opera House, Covent Garden and was broadcast by the BBC. A number of years previously a conversation with Fr. Malachy had left an impression on the young composer: "I remember asking Father Malachy what Thérèse of Lisieux did, and he said, 'She didn't do anything. But what she does now is a different matter.'"[13]

Fr. Malachy's Funeral Mass

Fr. Malachy Lynch passed away on Friday, 5 May 1972. The main celebrant for his funeral Mass was his brother, Kilian Lynch who had been Prior General of the Carmelite Order from 1947 to 1959. The official account of the funeral details those clergy who attended:

> Fr Kilian Lynch offered the Mass of Requiem. About seventy other priests joined in its celebration, among them Fr. Sean Coughlan, Assistant General, Fr. H. A. Brennan, Provincial and Fr J. L. Ryan, Provincial, Irish Province. His Grace the Archbishop of Southwark, Most Rev. Cyril Cowderoy presided. The President of Ireland, His Excellency Mr E. de Valera was represented at the Mass, also Rt. Rev. Dr. Say, Anglican Bishop of Rochester. Carmelites from the English and Welsh houses were present and among Carmelites from Ireland were Fr W. P. Russell, Fr T. A. Walsh, Fr T. E. Devane, and Fr J. V. Sugrue.[14]

In addition to the Requiem Mass at Aylesford, there was also a memorial Mass for Malachy Lynch at Saint George's Cathedral, Southwark on the morning of 17 June, once again a mark of the man's popularity.[15]

The Little Requiem

John Tavener was moved to write his *Little Requiem for Father Malachy Lynch* because he knew the Carmelite personally and was deeply influ-

---

11. *Ibid.*, p. 28.
12. *Ibid.*
13. *Ibid.*, p. 29.
14. *Bulletin*, p. 1.
15. *Bulletin*, p. 6.

enced by him. But the composer was also inspired by the thunder storm which blitzed the open-air funeral Mass.

The *Little Requiem* was written extremely quickly and received its first performance at Winchester Cathedral as part of the Southern Cathedrals Festival only two months after its completion; during the time of its composition Tavener visited the Carmelites at Allington to share his thoughts concerning the new work.[16] The conductor at the first performance was the Organist and Master of the Choristers at Winchester, Martin Neary, who later went on to record the work with the choir of Westminster Abbey. One cannot help imagining how much Fr. Malachy would have loved the setting: the great medieval cathedral of Winchester! The work was again performed in 1973 at the Queen Elizabeth Hall in London's Southbank Centre.

The *Little Requiem* is very simple, written in several parts and is mostly in unison or octaves. There is no counterpoint (i.e. interplay of voices), the music being rather vertical in its orientation. The work is in *parlando* ("speaking") style, meaning that even as the words are being sung, they should sound like they are being spoken and clearly enunciated. The voices of the choir are accompanied by a chamber orchestra of two flutes, trumpet, strings and organ. Tavener set only four sections of the Requiem Mass: *Requiem aeternam, Dies irae, Lacrymosa – Dies irae* and *Libera me*. The *Requiem aeternam* is repeated at the end. Tavener notes at the beginning of the score:

> Father Malachy was responsible for the re-founding of the Carmelite Priory at Aylesford, Kent, where he was Prior. I began the *Requiem* on returning from his dramatic open-air funeral; the music has for me a deeply personal connection with Father Malachy, hence the use of the Latin singular throughout.[17]

The *Requiem aeternam* of Tavener's setting is at once ethereal, other-worldly, intimate, and tender. There is a real sense of the coming together of heaven and earth. He achieves maximum effect with the most modest of means – the sign of a great composer – repeating, again and again, a seven-note motif which came into his head while attending the funeral at Aylesford.

The *Dies irae* is a truly terrifying piece. One can hear the thunder from

---

16.   Mc Greal, *A Stumbling Pilgrim*, p. 132.

17.   John Tavener, *Little Requiem for Father Malachy Lynch* (London: Chester Music, 1995). After the first performances Tavener was encouraged to expand the *Little Requiem* into a complete *Office of the Dead*. This expanded version was initially scored for six soloists and orchestra. Six years later Tavener revised it for soloists, six-part choir and orchestra. Arguably, however, the original *Little Requiem* is more directly affecting then the later expansions.

the funeral at Aylesford in the music as the notes literally flash forth! The use of the organ in this part of the score is no less thunderous. The organist is directed to use the most powerful bass registers of the instrument. This is contrasted with moments of extreme tenderness with use of harmony reminiscent of French composers such as Francis Poulenc and Maurice Duruflé, both of whom were outstanding choral composers. The choir harmony alternates with exquisite brief interludes either on flutes or strings.

The *Libera me* returns to the thunderous mood before yielding once again to the gentleness of the *Requiem aeternam.*

The *Little Requiem for Father Malachy Lynch* is a small masterpiece of the modern choral repertoire which deserves to be better known. In it the composer avoids all ostentation in his desire to pay fitting tribute to a great man and a great Carmelite.

10

Carmel and Music: List of Available Recordings

The following list is intended to be a non-exhaustive and yet representative catalogue of recordings, indicating some of those most readily available in a variety of formats today. The recording date and release date are given in square brackets. Occasionally only the recording or the release date is available.

Chapter 1 – Carmel and Music in the Middle Ages and Renaissance

Le Chant des Templiers, Ensemble Organum, Marcel Pérès (Ambroisie: AM9997). [2005, 2006]

Every Delight and Fair Pleasure: The Music of Northern Italy, The Ensemble of the Fourteenth Century, John Griffiths and John Stinson (Move Records: MD 3092) – includes the madrigals, *La douce Cere*, *Le aurate chiome*, *Alba columba* and *Imperial sedendo* and the ballate *Serva ziascuno, Sempre dona t'amai* and *Non corer troppo* by Bartolino da Padova, O. Carm. [1991, 1991]

Music for a Medieval Banquet, The Newberry Consort, Mary Springfels, Judith Malafronte, Drew Minter (Harmonia Mundi: HCX 3957038) – includes *Alba columba* of Bartolino da Padova, O. Carm. [1990, 1993]

Ballate e Madrigali, Concentus Lucensis, Cantilena Antiqua, Stefano Albarello (Tactus: TC400002) – includes *Ama chi t'ama* of Bartolino da Padova, O. Carm. The same recording includes the following music of John Hothby (Johannes Octoboni), O. Carm.: *Diva panthera, Tard il mio cor, Ave sublime triumphale, Amor.* [2001, 2002]

Rosa e orticha: Music of the Trecento, Ensemble Syntama, Alexandre Danilevski (Carpe Diem: CD 16287) – includes *El no mi giova, I bei sembianti, Dulce cere* and *Alba colonba* of Bartolino da Padova, O. Carm. [2010, 2012]

Ars subtilior, Catherine Bott, The New London Consort, Philip Pickett (Linn: CKD 039) – includes *La douce cere* by Bartolino da Padova, O. Carm., as well as *La dolce sere* from the Codex Faenza. [rel. 1998]

Codex Faenza: Instrumental Music of the Early 15th Century, Ensemble Unicorn, Michael Posch (Naxos: 8.553618). [1995, 2007]

Gothic Pipes: The Earliest Organ Music, Kimberley Marshall (organist), Cappella Romana (plainchant) (Loft Recordings: LRCD-1047) – includes *Kyrie cunctipotens genitor Deus, Bel fiore dança* and *Or sus, vous dormés trop* from the *Codex Faenza*. [rec. 1985]

The First Printed Organ Music, Arnolt Schlick 1512, Kimberley Marshall (organist) (Loft Recordings: LRCD-1124) – includes the organ pieces *Was ich durch Glück* and *Zucht eer und lob* by Paul Hofhaimer, the Fugger-organist at the Carmelite church in Augsburg. [1991, 2012]

Chapter 2 – Frei Manuel Cardoso, O. Carm.

Frei Manuel Cardoso, Requiem, The Tallis Scholars, Peter Phillips (Gimell: CDGIM 021) – in addition to Cardoso's setting of the Requiem Mass, this recording includes *Non mortui, Sitivit anima mea, Mulier quae erat, Nos autem gloriari, Versa est luctum, Credo quod redemptor, Vivo ego, dicit Dominus, Ave Maria.* [rel. 1990]

Manuel Cardoso, Sitivit Anima Mea, Tulerunt Lapides Ut Lacerent In Eum, Non Mortui Qui Sunt In Inferno, Missa Regina Caeli, Duarte Lôbo, Audivi Vocem De Caelo, Pater Peccavi, Missa Pro Defunctis à 8, The Sixteen, Harry Christophers (Collins Classics: 14072) [1993, 1994]

Portuguese Requiem Masses, Lôbo and Cardoso, Schola Cantorum Oxford, Jeremy Summerly (Naxos: 8.550682) [1992, 1993]

Portuguese Polyphony, Cardoso, Lôbo, Magalhães, Fonseca, Trosylho, Escobar, Ars Nova, Bo Holten (Naxos: 8.553310) – includes *Lamentatio* and *Magnificat secundi toni* by Cardoso. [1992, 1995]

Manuel Cardoso, Missa Misere Mihi Domine, Magnificat (Secundi toni), Ensemble Vocal Européen, Philippe Herreweghe (Harmonia Mundi France: HMC 901543) – includes the motets *Sitivit anima mea* and *Non mortui* of Cardoso. [1994, 1997]

Masterpieces of Portuguese Polyphony 2, Choir of Westminster Cathedral, James O'Donnell (Hyperion Helios: 55229) – includes *Non mortui, Sitivit anima mea, Mulier quae erat, Tulerunt lapides, Nos autem gloriari* and *Lamentatio* (for Maundy Thursday) by Cardoso. [1991, 1992]

Renaissance Portugal: Sacred Music of Cardoso and Lôbo, The Sixteen, Harry Christophers (Coro: COR16032) – includes Cardoso's *Sitivit anima mea, Tulerunt lapides, Non mortui* and *Missa Regina Caeli* and is a reissue of the Collins Classics recording listed above. [1993, 2007]

Paradisi portas: Music from 17th Century Portugal The Choir of the Queen's College, Oxford (Guild: GMCD 7296) – includes Cardoso's *Missa Paradisi Portas*, his motet *Paradisi Portas* and *Sitivit anima mea.* [2005, 2005]

Manuel Cardoso, Magnificat Octavi Toni, Magnificat Quinti Toni, Missa Secundi Toni, Motets with music by De Brito, Magalhães and Morago, Choir of Girton College, Cambridge, Historic Brass of the Royal Academy of Music, Gareth Wilson (Toccata Classics: TOCC 0476) – includes first recordings of new versions of Cardoso's *Sitivit anima mea* and *Non mortui.* [2017, 2018]

Manuel Cardoso: Requiem, Lamentations, Magnificat and Motets, Cupertinos, Luís Toscano (Hyperion: CDA68252) – includes Cardoso's *Lamentations, Requiem, Domine tu mihi lavas pedes?, Magnificat secundi toni a 4, Amen dico vobis, Cum audisset Johannes, Ipse est qui post me, Omnis vallis, Quid hic statis?, Tua est potentia, Sitivit anima mea.* [2019]

Amarae Morti: Music by Cardoso, Gombert, Lassus, Morales, Palestrina, Phinot, Victoria, El León de Oro, Peter Phillips (Hyperion: CDA68279) – includes Cardoso's *Lamentatio Feria quinta in Coena Domini – Lectio II.* [2019]

Chapter 3 – Benedictus of Saint Joseph (Buns), O. Carm.

Four Dutch composers of the Golden Age. Ensemble Bouzignac, Utrecht, Erik Van Nevel (Vanguard Classics: 99126) – includes *Magnificat* (Opus 5, no. 3), *O sors optata* (Opus 6, no. 9) and *Salve Regina* (Opus 1, no. 3) of Benedictus of St Joseph. [1995, 1996]

Benedictus Buns, Ensemble Severin, (NM Classics: 92131) – recording of Benedictus's thirteen instrumental triosonatas from *Orpheus Elianus* (1698). [2003, 2006]

Saints & Sinners, Cappella Figuralis, Jos van Veldhoven. (CCS 12498) – includes *Ave Maria* (Opus 9), *Domine, ne in furore* (Opus 6, no. 7) *Posita in media* (Opus 5, no. 5), *Obstupescite* (Opus 6, no. 12). [1998, 1998]

Chapter 4 – George Frederick Handel's *Music for the Carmelites*

Handel, Carmelite Vespers, 1707, Taverner Choir & Players, Andrew Parrott (Virgin Veritas: 7243 5 61579 2 7). [1989, 1999]

Handel, Caldara, Carmelite Vespers 1709, Roberta Invernizzi, Robin Johannsen, Martin Oro, Markus Brutscher, Antonio Abete, Academia Montis Regalis, Alessandro De Marchi (Deutsche Harmonia Mundi: 88691926042). [2011, 2012]

Handel, Dixit Dominus, Salve Regina, Laudate Pueri, Saeviat Tullus, Annick Massis, Magdalena Kožená, Les Musiciens du Louvre, Marc Minkowski. (Archiv Produktion: 459 627-2) [1998, 1999]

Chapter 5 – Felix Mendelssohn's Elijah

Mendelssohn, Elijah, Bryn Terfel, Renée Fleming, Patricia Bardon, John Mark Ainsley, Edinburgh Festival Chorus, Orchestra Of The Age Of Enlightenment, Paul Daniel (Decca: 455 688-2). [1996, 1997]

Chapter 6 – Ven. Augustine Mary of the Blessed Sacrament (Hermann Cohen, OCD)

Mass of Saint Teresa of Avila, Composed by Fr. Hermann Cohen, OCD. Sung Latin Mass by the Carmelite Choir, Kensington, London. (Ambrosian Singers and BBC.) Two additional Motets – *Flos Carmeli* (Flower of Carmel) and *Panis Vivus* (Living Bread). Conductor John McCarthy, OBE (Carmelite Book Service, Oxford Ref. 8842). [rec. 1984]

Chapter 7 – Francis Poulenc's *Dialogues des Carmélites*

Francis Poulenc, *Dialogues des Carmélites,* Denise Duval, Régine Crespin – Denise Scharley, Liliane Berton, Chœurs Et Orchestre Du Théâtre National De L'Opéra, Pierre Dervaux (Warner Classics: 50999 9 48228 2 3) – the classic recording of Poulenc's work. [1958, 1998]

Francis Poulenc, Dialogues des Carmélites, Catherine Dubosc, Rita Gorr, Rachel Yakar, Martine Dupuy, Brigitte Fournier, José Van Dam, Jean-Luc Viala, Orchestre De L'Opéra De Lyon, Kent Nagano (Virgin Classics: 0946 3 58657 2 1). [1990, 2006]

Chapter 8 – Sir Lennox Berkeley's *Four Poems by St. Teresa of Avila*

Kathleen Ferrier: Songs My Father Taught Me (Gala: GL 318) – this recording features a recording of the first performance of Berkeley's *Four Poems by Saint Teresa of Avila* with orchestra on 14 April 1948 with Kathleen Ferrier (contralto) and The English Chamber Orchestra conducted by Arnold Goldsbrough. [1948, 1997]

A Lennox Berkeley Centenary Album, Lennox Berkeley, Dennis Brain, Colin Horsley, Pamela Bowden, John Minchinton, Thomas Hemsley, Ernest Lush (EMI Classics: 7243 5 85138 2 0) – includes the recording of *Four Poems by Saint Teresa of Avila* by Pamela Bowden. [rel. 2003]

Lennox Berkeley, Piano Concerto, Four Poems by Teresa of Avila, Michael Berkeley, Tristessa, Gethsemane Fragment, Richard Hickox, Catherine Wyn-Rogers, Howard Shelley, BBC National Orchestra Of Wales (Chandos: CHAN 10265) – Volume 5 of The Berkeley Edition which includes works by Lennox Berkeley and his son, Michael. [2004, 2004]

Chapter 9 – Sir John Tavener's *Little Requiem for Father Malachy Lynch*

John Tavener, *Innocence*, Westminster Abbey Choir, Martin Neary – includes the *Little Requiem for Father Malachy Lynch,* (Sony Classical: SK 66613). [1994-1995, 1995]

Recommended Carmelite Websites

For more information about the Carmelites today, our spirituality and our ministries worldwide, visit:

carmelites.net

ocarm.org

carmelites.info

For a listing of Carmelite provinces worldwide, visit:

carmelites.info/provinces

For a listing of Monasteries of Carmelite nuns, visit:

carmelites.info/nuns

For a listing of Carmelite Hermitages, please visit:

carmelites.info/hermits

For a listing of sites about Lay Carmelites:

carmelites.info/lay carmel

For a listing of Affiliated Congregations and Institutes:

carmelites.info/congregations

For more information about our work with the United Nations, visit:

carmelitengo.org

For more information about other publications from Carmelite Media, visit:

carmelites.info/publications